BAPTISTWAY®

# Adult Bible Study Guide

# Amos, Hosea, Micah

Howard Batson
Dennis Foust
Gary Light

BAPTISTWAY PRESS®
Dallas, Texas

*Amos, Hosea, Micah—Adult Bible Study Guide*

Copyright © 2003 by BAPTISTWAY PRESS®.
All rights reserved.
Printed in the United States of America.

BAPTISTWAY PRESS® Management Team
Executive Director, Baptist General Convention of Texas: Charles Wade
Coordinator, Church Health and Growth Section: H. Lynn Eckeberger
Director, Bible Study/Discipleship Center: Dennis Parrott

Publishing consultant: Ross West, Positive Difference Communications
Cover and Interior Design and Production: Desktop Miracles, Inc.
Front Cover Photo: Samaria, BiblePlaces.com

First edition: June 2003
ISBN: 1–931060–35–5

# How to Make the Best Use of This Issue

Whether you're the teacher or a student—

1. Start early in the week before your class meets.
2. Overview the study. Look at the table of contents, read the study introduction, and read the unit introduction for the lesson you're about to study. Try to see how each lesson relates to the unit and overall study of which it is a part.
3. Use your Bible to read and consider prayerfully the Scripture passages for the lesson. (You'll see that each writer has chosen a favorite translation for each unit in this issue. You're free to use the Bible translation you prefer and compare it with the translation chosen for that unit, of course.)
4. After reading all the Scripture passages in your Bible, then read the writer's comments. The comments are intended to be an aid to your study of the Bible.
5. Read the small articles—"sidebars"—in each lesson. They are intended to provide additional, enrichment information and inspiration and to encourage thought and application.
6. Try to answer for yourself the questions included in each lesson. They're intended to encourage further thought and application, and they can also be used in the class session itself.

If you're the teacher—

A. Do all of the things just mentioned, of course.
B. In the first session of the study, briefly overview the study by identifying with your class the date on which each lesson will be studied. Lead your class to write the date in the table of contents on page 5 and on the first page of each lesson. You might also find it helpful to make and post a chart that indicates the date on which each lesson will be studied. If all of your class has e-mail, send them an e-mail with the dates the lessons will be studied.
C. You may want to get the enrichment teaching help that is provided in the *Baptist Standard* and/or on the internet. Call 214–630–4571 to begin your subscription to the *Baptist Standard*. Access the internet information by checking the *Baptist Standard* website at

http://www.baptiststandard.com. (Other class participants may find this information helpful, too.)

D.  Get a copy of the *Teaching Guide*, which is a companion piece to these lesson comments. It contains additional Bible comments plus two teaching plans. The teaching plans in the *Teaching Guide* are intended to provide practical, easy-to-use teaching suggestions that will work in your class.

E.  After you've studied the Bible passage, the lesson comments, and other material, use the teaching suggestions in the *Teaching Guide* to help you develop your plan for leading your class in studying each lesson.

F.  Enjoy leading your class in discovering the meaning of the Scripture passages and in applying these passages to their lives.

# Amos, Hosea, Micah

---

M I C A H

## *What the Lord Requires*

# Introducing

## AMOS: *A God Who Roars*

What kind of God do you believe in? Critics of religion have sometimes charged that religious people believe in a God created in their own image, a God they have fashioned for themselves to satisfy their desires. When the prophet Amos looked at the religion of the people of Israel in the mid-eighth century BC, Amos would have agreed with this assessment.

Amos saw much in the culture of his day that indicated that the god the people of Israel worshiped was not the true God. The people were greedy for luxury, prejudiced against the poor, and hungry for power. Thus they worshiped a god who did not mind whether they lived that way as long as they paid him proper homage in regular, beautiful worship services.

Such a god, however, was not the God who had taken Amos from "following the flock" and had commanded him to prophesy God's message (Amos 7:15).[1] For Amos, God could not be tamed to fit with human desires. The God whose message Amos delivered would not put a stamp of approval on the greed, prejudice, and power plays of human culture in exchange for elaborate sacrifices and regular attendance at the worship services. Amos's God was not a tame God. Indeed, the God whom Amos served was a God who "roars" (Amos 1:2). Amos said (3:8) that, like a lion, this God "has roared." Thus, "who can but prophesy?"

The Book of Amos is about the roaring of this God against God's own people. Amos, the first of the writing prophets, burst upon the eighth-century scene with a powerful and powerfully unpopular message from God. God was fed up with the people's mistreatment of the poor and the powerless, fed up with the luxurious living of some of the people at the expense of others, and fed up with these people's thinking they could get away with it if they just sprinkled a few grains of religion on their behavior. God's attitude was not based on whim, either. When God had entered into covenant with Israel centuries before this time, God had made clear the kind of behavior expected. Israel had simply disobeyed and had done so flagrantly. God's message was, *the end.* Because of their evil behavior, *the*

7

Additional Resources for Studying the Book of Amos:[2]

Donald E. Gowan. "Amos." *The New Interpreter's Bible.* Volume VII. Nashville: Abingdon Press, 1996.

James Limburg. *Hosea—Micah.* Interpretation: A Bible Commentary for Teaching and Preaching. Atlanta: John Knox Press, 1988.

Billy K. Smith. *Amos, Obadiah, Jonah.* The New American Commentary. Nashville: Broadman and Holman Publishers, 1995.

Ralph L. Smith. "Amos." *The Broadman Bible Commentary.* Volume 7. Nashville, Tennessee: Broadman Press, 1972.

Douglas Stuart. *Hosea—Jonah.* Word Biblical Commentary. Volume 31. Waco, Texas: Word Books, Publisher, 1987.

---

*end* was coming upon the nation of Israel. Israel could not count on some presumed special relationship with God to forestall it, either. So Amos cried (4:12): "Prepare to meet your God, O Israel." These words were a warning of the end.

So how do you think the God of Amos would relate to us and our culture? Do you see any parallels? If we ever understand Amos's message and see how it applies to us, we may also want to tell Amos, *Go back where you came from and prophesy there* (7:12). Frankly, we tend to want a god just like Israel had. We want to feel that God thinks a whole lot like us. We also want to feel that this God is *for* us and our ways. The idea that God may be *against* us because of our sins has never been popular, and today is no exception.

These desires of ours mean that the prophet Amos has a thing or two to say to us. We must pay attention if we truly want to know and serve the God of the Bible.

Five lessons comprise this study of the Book of Amos. Lesson one deals with Amos 1—2, which record Amos's magnificent sermon that came to a point on Israel itself. Lesson two considers Amos's message about the economic injustices that brought God's judgment on Israel. Lesson three treats the people's attempt to use worship services to fulfill their religious obligations when what God wanted was justice. Lesson four is on Amos's encounter with the religious leadership of the day who, allied with the government, rejected God's message. Lesson five focuses on the certainty of God's judgment on Israel plus the hope of restoration that God offered.

## AMOS: A GOD WHO ROARS

## NOTES

1. Unless otherwise indicated, all Scripture quotations in "Introducing Amos" and the lessons on Amos are from the New American Standard Bible®, copyright © The Lockman Foundation 1960, 1962, 1963, 1968, 1971, 1972, 1973, 1975, 1977, 1995. Used by permission.
2. Listing a book does not imply full agreement by the writers or BAPTISTWAY PRESS® with all of its comments.

## Focal Text
Amos 2:4–16

## Background
Amos 1—2

## Main Idea
We, like ancient Israel, must first be concerned about our sins, our acts of injustice, rather than being preoccupied with other's sins and acts of injustice.

## Question to Explore
Whose sin does God really want us to focus on?

## Study Aim
To acknowledge the need to focus on my sins and my part in our society's injustices

## Study and Action Emphases
- Affirm the Bible as our authoritative guide for life and ministry
- Develop a growing, vibrant faith
- Value all people as created in the image of God
- Obey and serve Jesus by meeting physical, spiritual, and emotional needs
- Equip people for servant leadership

# LESSON ONE

# It's for You

## Quick Read
The ancient Israelites were so focused on the sins of neighboring nations that they failed to see their sin of enriching themselves at the expense of the poor.

Do you remember in the story of Winnie the Pooh when Pooh Bear went into Rabbit's hole, and Rabbit asked him, "Would you like condensed milk or honey on your bread?"

Pooh said, "Never mind the bread!" Pooh just wanted the honey.

Well, the loveable bear ate and ate and ate. Finally, Rabbit gave in and just handed him the whole honey jar. Pooh moved on to another honey jar and yet another. He ate until all of Rabbit's honey was gone.

As the bloated bear tried to exit Rabbit's hole, he got his head out, but his hind end would not fit. "Oh bother," said Pooh Bear. "I'm stuck." Rabbit pushed from the rear. He didn't want Pooh Bear sticking out of his front door—the head outside the cave and the rear inside. But the honey-filled bear just wouldn't budge.

"This situation calls for an expert," Owl said.

Gopher popped up. With his characteristic lisp, he whistled, "Ssssomebody call for an exxxcavation exssspert?"

Christopher Robin finally arrived on the scene and explained that Pooh would just be stuck until he was thin again, implying that Pooh should not eat.

Days passed.

All of a sudden Gopher popped back up with a lunchbox. "A lunch box?" asked the wedged bear. By now, he had not eaten in a long, long, long time.

"It certainly issss," said Gopher. "Sssswing sssshift you know. Time for my midnight sssnack."

"What sort of lunch is in that lunch box?" asked Pooh Bear, desperately.

"Let's sssssee here," said Gopher. "Ssssummer ssquash, sssalmon sssalad, ssuccotash, and honey."

"Honey!" said Pooh Bear.

"Oh no," said Rabbit. He ran out the back door, trying to keep Pooh Bear from eating any more honey so he wouldn't clog up the entrance any longer than necessary.

Next, an interesting thing happened. I think Pooh Bear was just trying to relate to the rodent because he said this to Gopher as Gopher would say it, lisp and all: "Could you ssspare a sssmall sssmackerel?"

Gopher replied, with a quizzical look, "You ought to do sssomething about that ssspeech impediment, sssonny."

What is so ironic about the story is that while Gopher always spoke with his characteristic "whistles," he suggested that Pooh Bear needed to work on his speech impediment! What Gopher could not see in himself, he saw so clearly in Pooh Bear.[1]

Ancient Israel had Gopher's problem. They had the ability to see the sins of all the nations around them but were quite surprised to discover they had some sins of their own.

# Amos 2:4–16

4 Thus says the LORD,
"For three transgressions of Judah and for four
I will not revoke its punishment,
Because they rejected the law of the LORD
And have not kept His statutes;
Their lies also have led them astray,
Those after which their fathers walked.
5 "So I will send fire upon Judah
And it will consume the citadels of Jerusalem."
6 Thus says the LORD,
"For three transgressions of
Israel and for four I will not revoke its punishment,
Because they sell the righteous for money
And the needy for a pair of sandals.
7 "These who pant after the very dust of the earth on the head of the
helpless
Also turn aside the way of the humble;
And a man and his father resort to the same girl
In order to profane My holy name.
8 "On garments taken as pledges they stretch out beside every altar,
And in the house of their God they drink the wine of those who have
been fined.
9 "Yet it was I who destroyed the Amorite before them,
Though his height was like the height of cedars
And he was strong as the oaks;
I even destroyed his fruit above and his root below.
10 "It was I who brought you up from the land of Egypt,
And I led you in the wilderness forty years
That you might take possession of the land of the Amorite.
11 "Then I raised up some of your sons to be prophets
And some of your young men to be Nazirites.
Is this not so, O sons of Israel?" declares the LORD.
12 "But you made the Nazirites drink wine,

And you commanded the prophets saying, 'You shall not prophesy!'
13 "Behold, I am weighted down beneath you
As a wagon is weighted down when filled with sheaves.
14 "Flight will perish from the swift,
And the stalwart will not strengthen his power,
Nor the mighty man save his life.
15 "He who grasps the bow will not stand his ground,
The swift of foot will not escape,
Nor will he who rides the horse save his life.
16 "Even the bravest among the warriors will flee naked in that day,"
declares the LORD.

## Seven Sermons Against Seven Sinful Nations (1:1—2:5)

If Amos had been a major league pitcher, he would not have been the master of the fast ball. The change-up would not have been his best bet. Rather, he would have been the curveball king. When a pitcher throws a curveball, the batter thinks the ball is headed in one direction. Then, suddenly, the ball takes a turn in a new, unexpected direction. Amos was a curveball pitcher.

In Amos 1:1, this prophetic pitcher stepped up on the mound. He was from Tekoa, a small rural Judean village about ten miles south of Jerusalem. The text tells us he was "among the sheepherders." The word here probably means that he was a manager of shepherds. Also, from 7:14 we learn that he was a cultivator of sycamore figs. Apart from these sermons, we really know very little about Amos. We don't know whether he was married or had any children. There is a lot more about Amos that we do not know than we do know.

*Ancient Israel . . . had the ability to see the sins of all the nations around them but were quite surprised to discover they had some sins of their own.*

We can be sure, though, that Amos had been called by God to carry a word to the nations. His ministry, despite the fact that he was from Judah in the south, was to Israel in the north. The people of God had been divided into two nations for almost 200 years by the time Amos began his preaching around 760 BC. His ministry took place during the most prosperous days of ancient Israel, during the reign of King Jeroboam II (reigned 786–746 BC; see 2 Kings 14:23–30; Hosea 1:1). Uzziah was on the throne in the Southern Kingdom in Jerusalem at the same time (reigned 783–742 BC; see 2 Chronicles 26; Isaiah 1:1; 6:1; Hosea 1:1).

During this prosperous time in Israel's history, many assumed they were enjoying the blessings of God. Like a roaring lion (1:2), however, God was ready to pounce on his people, ancient Israel (compare 3:4, 8).

Before God pounced on God's own people, though, Amos began preaching to the various nations surrounding ancient Israel. Amos prophesied against the sinful bordering nations as if he were preaching around the points of the compass. He proceeded: Aram in the northeast (1:3–5); Philistia in the southwest (1:6–8); Tyre to the northwest (1:9–10); and Edom in the southeast (1:11–12).[2] More importantly, however, we note the movement of the sermons as they began with foreign

*Like the bully on the grade school playground, the rich were pushing the poor aside if they sought justice . . . .*

nations (Aram, Philistia, and Tyre) and moved toward blood relatives (Edom, 1:11–12; Ammon, 1:13–15; and Moab, 2:1–3), until the last of the seven oracles is aimed at the sister kingdom of Judah (2:4–5). Strategically, the prophet was moving closer to his real mark, the Northern Kingdom.

Each of these seven sermons against the nations followed a common pattern:

(1) They begin with the introductory formula, "Thus says the Lord" (see 1:3, 6, 9, 11, 13; 2:1, 4).
(2) Next comes a statement of the certainty of judgment, "For three transgressions of . . . and for four" (see 1:3, 6, 9, 11, 13; 2:1, 4).
(3) Specific charges of guilt follow.
(4) The pronouncement of punishment comes next.
(5) Four of the sermons close with the formula "says the Lord" or "says the Lord God" (1:5, 8, 15; 2:3)

Using the sermon aimed at Judah as an example, we can see how the prophet employed this common pattern. He began with the introductory formula (2:4), "Thus says the Lord," and then immediately gave the statement of the certainty of judgment, "For three transgressions of Judah and for four I will not revoke its punishment." According to the specific charge of guilt, we see that Judah, the Southern Kingdom, had broken the law that God had given them. Judah, unlike some of the other peoples, was not chastised for being oppressive against foreign nations.

Rather, Judah had disobeyed the commandments God had given to Moses on Mount Sinai. When Amos declared that the inhabitants of Judah rejected the Torah, the law, he was probably referring to the Ten Commandments and, more broadly, the whole first five books of the Bible.

The punishment that would follow for the Southern Kingdom was fire. Just as for the other nations, God declared that fire would be used against God's own people. Their breaking the covenant with their Lord is placed side by side with the sins of the foreign nations who went so far as to sell people into slavery.

## One Sermon Against God's Sinful People (2:6–8)

As Amos drew attention to the sins of Israel's enemies, his audience would have been delighted. When he even had the courage to preach against his own people (remember, Amos was from Judah), they must have been ecstatic! When the seventh sermon, the sermon against Judah, was complete, the Israelites assumed the prophet was finished. Seven is the biblical number for completeness and finality. Notice that the statement of certain judgment adds up to seven—three sins plus four sins (1:3, 6, 9, 11, 13; 2:1, 4). Like Gopher, who heard clearly Pooh's lisp but ignored his own, Israel was unaware that it had any sins the prophet might address.

*During this prosperous time in Israel's history, many assumed they were enjoying the blessings of God.*

Imagine the surprised look on the faces of Amos's audience when he started preaching an eighth sermon, beginning with the familiar formula, "Thus says the Lord" (2:6). He had already prophesied against seven other nations. *Who's next? What is he talking about? This sermon is over,* the Israelites must have thought to themselves.

When Amos said the name "Israel," the name of his audience, it must have hit like a clap of thunder. The Israelites had focused on the failures of the other nations and never imagined their own name would be mentioned. They had already sung the hymn of invitation and were ready to go home!

Amos followed his familiar pattern: "For three transgressions of Israel and for four, I will not revoke its punishment" (2:6). The specific charges come next (2:6–8). By using the formula employed against Israel's enemies,

Amos was saying that Israel would be held accountable to God just as all the other nations would.

We can imagine that the *Amens* stopped and the *Oh, me's* started. What about us? Could it be that each of us thinks that somehow God is going to make a special exception in regard to our life, in regard to our sin? Amos was saying that God was sovereign over all the nations, over all creation, and that God was sovereign over the Northern Kingdom as well. God would call God's own people into account for their sins.

Look at what Israel had done to deserve judgment. First, Israel was charged with putting a price tag on human lives (2:6). While

*We must stop focusing on sins that are beyond our backyard and look at our own acts of greed and injustice.*

we cannot be certain, perhaps Amos was referring to corrupt judges who were accepting bribes and deciding cases against the poor. Or perhaps Amos was speaking of a practice by which moneylenders were foreclosing on small loans they had extended to the poor. By using the phrase about selling "the needy for a pair of sandals," the prophet was indicating the ridiculously low price for which the well-to-do, those in positions of power, were willing to turn their backs on the downtrodden. The corrupt court should stop aiding the rich by taking advantage of the poor and selling them into slavery. God's people should always remember that they

## The Sermon on the Mount

Making his way up a hill in order to teach, Jesus told his followers about the kingdom of God. He declared that each disciple would do well to focus on his own sins before he began to think about the sins of others (Matthew 7:1–5). We must fight our tendency to minimize our faults while we exaggerate others' faults. We must clear up our rosy view of ourselves and remove our jaundiced view of those around us.

A tenant complained to the landlord, "The people upstairs are getting on my nerves. Last night they stomped and banged on the floor after midnight."

The landlord inquired, "Did it wake you up?"

"No," the tenant replied. "I just happened to be up practicing my tuba."

What Jesus is really saying is that only those who are willing to submit to judgment themselves are qualified to judge. Only those who have the logs taken out of their eyes can see clearly enough to remove the speck from someone else's eye (Matthew 7:5).

themselves were freed from slavery by the Exodus from Egypt, and they were always to have mercy on the needy.

Second, the prophet illustrated the position of the poor by saying that the rich were trampling upon them (2:7). Using the courts to pervert justice, the rich were, literally, treating the poor like dirt. Like the bully on the grade school playground, the rich were pushing the poor aside if they sought justice at the gate of the city (2:7; see Exodus 23:6; Proverbs 17:23).

The third accusation concerns both a man and his father having sexual relations with the same girl (2:7). Most likely, the abused girl was a slave who was being pressured to extend sexual favors to the men of the household. For both the father and the son to sleep with the same slave girl would be a breach of the covenant (Ex.21:7–11; Leviticus 18:7–8; 19:20–22).

*. . . Amos was saying that Israel would be held accountable to God just as all the other nations would.*

Fourth, we note that the creditors were not returning garments to the owners at sunset (2:8). These garments had been used as collateral for loans. By law, the poor were to receive back their garments so that they might have some protection against the cold night air (Ex. 22:26–27; Deuteronomy 24:12–13).

Finally, Amos accused Israel of drinking wine that had been paid by those who were satisfying a fine. The rich were getting richer at the expense of the poor.

## God's Goodness to Israel (2:9–12)

Unlike ancient Israel, who oppressed the poor, God had been working on behalf of his people. As a result of God's helpful hand, Israel had been established as a nation. The use of the pronoun "I" is emphatic in the Hebrew language: "I" destroyed; "I" brought you up. Verses 10–11 lists the things God had done to establish God's people Israel (2:9–11).

*The Israelites had focused on the failures of the other nations and never imagined their own name would be mentioned.*

The "Amorite" refers to the inhabitants of Palestine before God's people occupied the land. They had a reputation for being strong giants (Numbers 13:28, 31–32). God said the Amorites had the "height of cedars" and were "strong as the oaks" (Amos 2:9). Notice, however, that they were totally destroyed all the way from the "fruit" to the "root" (2:9). Israel should beware of God's willingness to completely destroy the Amorites because of their moral decay.

Second, Amos referred to the Exodus of Israel from Egypt. God liberated the Israelites from slavery and brought them up to give them the land God had promised to their forefathers. When we look at the Old Testament, the Exodus from Egypt was the most important event in all the history of God's people.

Third, God had led Israel through the desert for forty years (2:10). Fourth, God had given them the gift of leaders. Prophets were called to proclaim the message, and Nazarites were called to live as examples of devotion to God. Remember, the Nazarites could not cut their hair, have contact with the dead, or drink alcoholic beverages. (Samson and Samuel are examples; see Judges 13:5, 7; 16:17; 1 Samuel 1:11.) But Israel's response (Amos 2:12) was to prevent the Nazarites from holy living and to silence the prophets who were providing God's word.

*The rich were getting richer at the expense of the poor.*

## God's Response to Israel's Rebellion (2:14–16)

The Northern Kingdom expected that when the great day of the Lord came it would yield positive results for them. It would be a day of judgment against Israel's enemies. To their surprise, they learned that the day would not bring the long-awaited deliverance but rather destruction upon God's people.

We are provided with a detailed account of military devastation awaiting ancient Israel on "that day," the day of the Lord (see Amos 5:18–20). The swift of Israel would not be fast enough to escape. The strong would not have enough strength to be able to stand. Even the bravest warriors would flee away naked in the day of God's judgment; they would drop their weapons and run.

## Implications for Today

The ancient Israelites were taken to task by God because they were so busy focusing on the sins of the other nations that they failed to recognize their

# Case Study

A church employee needed an extended leave of absence due to an infection. The employee was honest and hard-working. The personnel policy called for ten days of sick leave, but this employee needed four months away from the job. Workers Compensation could not help because the absence was unrelated to work. Disability insurance would not help for months. The employee was a single father trying to raise his family with his meager salary.

The personnel committee faced some tough decisions. Should they ignore the policy and extend additional months of sick leave? Should they grant a leave of absence without pay, realizing that he would never be able to take care of his family? Should they continue to pay the employee? What would you decide to do if you were a member of this church's committee? What would you do if this employee worked for your business?

---

own acts of injustice against the poor. Their own greed and materialistic hearts had led them to trample on the poor.

We also have a tendency to "shorten the sin list," eliminating our sins from it. We live with a national economy that is based on our insatiable appetites for more. We are privileged to live in the richest, most powerful nation on earth. We police other nations without their consent, employ their workers for a fraction of what we pay our own, and throw away more food every year as Americans than some small nations produce.

We must stop focusing on sins that are beyond our backyard and look at our own acts of greed and injustice. If we don't, we too stand to suffer the wrath of God as ancient Israel did.

## QUESTIONS

1. Why do you think we have a tendency to focus on the sins of others rather than our own failures?

2. In what ways do we take advantage of the poor and needy without even realizing it?

3. Why did Amos use the same prophetic formula to address ancient Israel that he did to address the seven other nations? What was he trying to communicate by saving the message against Israel as the last in the sermon?

4. What charges might Amos bring against the American culture?

## NOTES

1. *The Many Adventures of Winnie the Pooh* (Home Video Version), The Walt Disney Company. This is a condensed version of the dialogue and description of events.
2. Douglas Stuart, *Hosea—Jonah*, Word Biblical Commentary, vol. 31 (Waco, Texas: Word Books, Publisher, 1987), 291. See also Billy K. Smith, *Amos, Obadiah, Jonah*, The New American Commentary (Nashville: Broadman and Holman Publishers, 1995), 59–69.

**Focal Text**

Amos 3:9—4:3; 5:10–15;
6:4–7; 8:4–6

**Background**

Amos 3:1—4:3; 5:1–17;
6:1–14; 8:4–14

**Main Idea**

God condemns economic
practices that mistreat the
poor and powerless.

**Question to
Explore**

Does God care about
economics?

**Study Aim**

To identify economic practices that God
condemns and how these apply to current life

**Study and Action Emphases**

- Affirm the Bible as our authoritative guide
  for life and ministry
- Develop a growing, vibrant faith
- Value all people as created in the image of
  God
- Obey and serve Jesus by meeting physical,
  spiritual, and emotional needs

# LESSON TWO

# Judgment on Injustice

## Quick Read

The wealthy citizens of Israel were mistreating
the poor in order to fulfill their insatiable desire
for more. Amos declared that their idea of
security, which was founded in riches, would
disappoint them as they faced God's judgment.

John and Roberta were touring their brand new house. Roberta had paid for the house with her money, a fact of which she constantly reminded John. In each room of the house she said to her husband: "John, if it were not for my money, we would not be here." John didn't say a word.

That afternoon a truck delivered a load of new furniture—furniture that Roberta had paid for with her money. After the furniture was in place, they toured the house again. As they observed each room, beautifully appointed and magnificently decorated, Roberta reminded her husband: "John, if it were not for my money, this furniture would not be here." Again, John was silent.

Late in the afternoon another truck came with a special piece of furniture that was to be the focal point of the family room. It was a combination stereo-television-computer center all wrapped into one gorgeous piece of furniture. When it was in place, Roberta again said: "John, if it were not for my money, this state-of-the-art electronics system would not be here."

Finally, John spoke: "Honey, I don't want to make you feel bad, but if it were not for your money, I wouldn't be here either!"

Money—whether we have it or we don't—can have great impact on our lives. In this Bible lesson, we see that God despises the *haves* when they take advantage of the *have-nots*. Amos evaluated the economic practices of ancient Israel and drew several conclusions.

## Amos 3:9–15

⁹Proclaim on the citadels in Ashdod and on the citadels in the land of Egypt and say, "Assemble yourselves on the mountains of Samaria and see the great tumults within her and the oppressions in her midst. ¹⁰"But they do not know how to do what is right," declares the LORD, "these who hoard up violence and devastation in their citadels."

¹¹ Therefore, thus says the Lord GOD,
"An enemy, even one surrounding the land,
Will pull down your strength from you
And your citadels will be looted."

¹² Thus says the LORD,
"Just as the shepherd snatches from the lion's mouth a couple of legs
    or a piece of an ear,
So will the sons of Israel dwelling in Samaria be snatched away—
With the corner of a bed and the cover of a couch!

13 "Hear and testify against the house of Jacob,"
    Declares the Lord GOD, the God of hosts.
14 "For on the day that I punish Israel's transgressions,
    I will also punish the altars of Bethel;
    The horns of the altar will be cut off
    And they will fall to the ground.
15 "I will also smite the winter house together with the summer house;
    The houses of ivory will also perish
    And the great houses will come to an end,"
    Declares the LORD.

# Amos 4:1–3

1 Hear this word, you cows of Bashan who are on the mountain of
    Samaria,
    Who oppress the poor, who crush the needy,
    Who say to your husbands, "Bring now, that we may drink!"
2 The Lord GOD has sworn by His holiness,
    "Behold, the days are coming upon you
    When they will take you away with meat hooks,
    And the last of you with fish hooks.
3 "You will go out through breaches in the walls,
    Each one straight before her,
    And you will be cast to Harmon," declares the LORD.

# Amos 5:10–15

10 They hate him who reproves in the gate,
    And they abhor him who speaks with integrity.
11 Therefore because you impose heavy rent on the poor
    And exact a tribute of grain from them,
    Though you have built houses of well-hewn stone,
    Yet you will not live in them;
    You have planted pleasant vineyards, yet you will not drink their wine.
12 For I know your transgressions are many and your sins are great,
    You who distress the righteous and accept bribes
    And turn aside the poor in the gate.
13 Therefore at such a time the prudent person keeps silent, for it is an evil
    time.
14 Seek good and not evil, that you may live;

And thus may the LORD God of hosts be with you,
Just as you have said!
15 Hate evil, love good,
And establish justice in the gate!
Perhaps the LORD God of hosts
May be gracious to the remnant of Joseph.

# Amos 6:4–7

4 Those who recline on beds of ivory
And sprawl on their couches,
And eat lambs from the flock
And calves from the midst of the stall,
5 Who improvise to the sound of the harp,
And like David have composed songs for themselves,
6 Who drink wine from sacrificial bowls
While they anoint themselves with the finest of oils,
Yet they have not grieved over the ruin of Joseph.
7 Therefore, they will now go into exile at the head of the exiles,
And the sprawlers' banqueting will pass away.

# Amos 8:4–6

4Hear this, you who trample the needy, to do away with the humble of the land, 5saying,
"When will the new moon be over,
So that we may sell grain,
And the sabbath, that we may open the wheat market,
To make the bushel smaller and the shekel bigger,
And to cheat with dishonest scales,
6 So as to buy the helpless for money
And the needy for a pair of sandals,
And that we may sell the refuse of the wheat?"

## False Sense of Security (3:9—4:3)

Amos called for two foreign nations to witness the violence in Samaria (3:9–15). For Israel to be condemned by the testimony of people from Egypt and Ashdod would be a humiliating experience. Ashdod was one of the cities of the Philistines.

The rich had become accustomed to exploiting the poor to support their opulent lifestyle. Because of this, the Lord said that the rich could no longer determine right from wrong (3:10).

With the flair of self-assured arrogance, Israel was certain of its position and power. This security, however, was without a foundation. An enemy, a foreign nation, would surround the land and plunder its fortresses (3:11). Like a lamb devoured into scraps, Samaria would be utterly destroyed (3:12). Even their religious security would be pulled out from under them (3:14), and their lavish houses would be demolished (3:15).

*Amos evaluated the economic practices of ancient Israel and drew several conclusions.*

In 4:1–3, moreover, Amos declared that the women, whom he referred to as the "cows of Bashan" and who had oppressed the poor and yet demanded still more, would be carried off "with meat hooks" and "fish hooks." Bashan was a fertile plain in the mountain range of both sides of the middle and upper Yarmuk River. The region was noted for lush pastures and, thus, the fattest of cattle. Amos was charging that the women had gained their wealthy condition by starving the poor.

The "meat hooks" and "fish hooks" referred to the appearance of the shackles to be put on the women as they were led into captivity. This humiliation would bring an end to the self-centered and consuming lifestyle of Israel's rich citizens. Israel's security was based on false illusions of grandeur. God's justice would put an end to their oppressive acts and thus their opulent lifestyle.

As they crushed the needy, the wealthy wives commanded their husbands, *Bring me more!* They needed more and more to satisfy their materialistic thirst. Their husbands further exploited the poor to keep their well-to-do wives happy and content.

In 6:1–7, Amos further reaffirmed that those who lived in high cotton were going to find themselves exiled from their land with barely the clothes on their back. Those who had slept on beds of ivory would not even have a mat on which to rest. Their security was false, indeed.

## Injustice Toward the Poor (5:10–15)

The great disparity between the *haves* and the *have-nots* in Israel was the result of unjust acts against the poor. In verses 10–13, Amos named these ways the rich were making life unbearable for the poor:

(1) Business leaders were manipulating justice through engaging in bribery, providing false witnesses, and intimidating judges (5:10, 12). The expression "in the gate" refers to judicial proceedings since cases were argued at the city gate (see Ruth 4:1–12).

(2) The rich were charging exorbitant rental fees for the use of the land. Thus, the farmer became a tenant, and the greatest share of the grain went to the urban landlord (Amos 5:11).

Amos warned the rich that they should not be so sure of their success. The oppressors who had taken from the poor in order to build their fine houses and plant their lush vineyards would not be allowed to enjoy what they had built or planted by breaking the backs of the poor (5:11).

## Great Disparity Between Rich and Poor (6:4–7)

A great disparity existed between the level of living of the rich and that of the poor. Amos was a preacher who had courage. Remember, he was prophesying around 760 BC, during the time of Jeroboam II, the height of the prosperity of the Northern Kingdom. Folks had assumed that their prosperity was the result of the direct blessing of God. The rich were living in opulence.

The disparity between rich and poor was evident in every detail of life (6:4–6). First, the wealthy citizens slept in the best beds, while the poor slept on a mat, at best. The word here for "sprawlers" has the connotation of drunkenness or laziness, indicating that they were hanging over the couches.

*They were so self-centered, so totally preoccupied with the pleasures of life, that they were blinded to the threatening reality all around them.*

Second, ordinary citizens in that day perhaps ate meat two or three times a year at the annual festivals. But the rich Israelites were taking the best calves from the midst of the fattening pen.

Third, the wealthy lounged around making up songs—imagining themselves to be little Davids, little kings (6:5). *You strum away,* Amos said, *on your harps* (6:5, author's paraphrase).

Fourth, they had the finest lotions, the best grade of oils for anointing. Whether the anointing was medicinal, cosmetic, or cultic, they had the very best at their disposal.

# Like a Devoured Lamb

Even the best shepherds could not protect every lamb from every wild beast. Losses were expected. A shepherd, however, was required to retrieve the remaining body parts, the scraps of the lamb, after a wild beast had devoured its prey (Exodus 22:10–13). By demonstrating how the animal was killed, the shepherd would not be responsible for the animal's loss. Amos was saying that through the judgment of God, ancient Israel would be destroyed like livestock devoured by a lion (Amos 3:12).

"Joseph," meaning Israel, was about to break up as a nation, and yet the leading citizens were not in distress as they should have been. They were so self-centered, so totally preoccupied with the pleasures of life, that they were blinded to the threatening reality all around them. According to them, life could not be better. According to Amos, it could not have been worse.

In America, as in ancient Israel, there is a great disparity between the *haves* and *have-nots.* As we began the twenty-first century, CEOs earned more than 400 times what their average workers made. As recently as 1980, that number was 40 times. Compare this to Japanese and German CEOs who earn only about 20 times as much as their average workers. Michael Eisner of Disney made $575 million in 1998. Compare that to the meager wage of the average Disney World employee who makes, in relative scale, pennies selling Mickey Mouse hats.[1] Isn't there something wrong in our value system when the general is making an average of 400 times more than the soldiers?

Not only do we have inequalities within our nation, but also when we compare our country to other countries, we really see the disparity that exists in the modern world. The reality is that the poorest 10 percent of Americans are still better off than two-thirds of the world's population. Recent research shows a staggering increase in global economic inequality. A wide-ranging study covering 85 percent of the world's population from 91 countries found that the richest 1 percent of the world's population has income equivalent to the poorest 57 percent

> *Amos warned the rich that they should not be so sure of their success.*

> *Israel's security was based on false illusions of grandeur.*

of the population combined. Four-fifths of the world's population live below what North America and Europe consider the poverty line.[2] The average North American consumes five times more than the average Mexican, ten times more than the average Chinese, and thirty times more than a person from India.[3]

*Unlike ancient Israel, we must never forget the poor, including the poorly-paid worker.*

Could we be the rich folk, the "cows of Bashan"? America's 102 million households, mine included, currently contain and consume more stuff than all other households throughout history, put together.[4] Yet most Americans don't really think of themselves as affluent.[5]

## Hypocrisy in Religion (8:4–6)

While the merchants of Israel were trampling the needy (8:4–6), the tradition of God's people was supposed to be one of an open hand toward the poor. God's law had outlined ways for the poor to regain self-respect and independence (see Exodus 22:21–27; Deuteronomy 16:11–14; 24:17–22).

While the merchants' formal piety caused them to cease selling on the Sabbath and other religious holidays, they inwardly despaired of any day on which they could not satisfy their greed by turning a profit. They also used other repulsive techniques to enrich themselves, including dishonest weights and measures, and chaff substituted for wheat. Honest weights

# Case Study

Consider a few questions that will have even greater impact if you have significant responsibilities in a company. Arrive at your answers in light of both what actually happens and how you think Amos would respond.

- Who gets the bonuses? Just the highest-ranking people?
- When the work team wins, do the bonuses go all the way down to every employee who is a member of the team?
- Whom do you think about when things go well? Do you reward only the guy steering the boat or all those who are breaking their backs rowing in the hot belly of the ship?
- Just because you *can* pay an employee a minimum wage, *should* you, in view of kingdom economics?

and measures were the requirements of God's law (Leviticus 19:35–36; Deut. 25:13–15; Proverbs 11:1; 16:11; 20:10). As a result of double-dealing, these merchants were able to "buy the helpless for money and the needy for a pair of sandals" (8:6). The meaning is that as their debts mounted up, the poor were finally forced to sell themselves into slavery (8:5–6).

We might ask, *What does that have to do with us? What does that have to do with America? We have not made ourselves wealthy at the expense of the poor.* Have we not? Do I bear no social responsibility for buying my child one more toy made in a sweat shop overseas where someone else's child slaves away in a living hell—just so mine might have one more plastic plaything? Just how many such things will be necessary to satisfy the consumer's appetite in our world?

> *Not only do we have inequalities within our nation, but also when we compare our country to other countries, we really see the disparity that exists in the modern world.*

A Thai toy factory became an inescapable inferno for hundreds of women who made a meager living in the firetrap. This factory was like many throughout the developing world where cheap labor is engaged to make millions of plastic toys for American children. Ironically, the single mothers who died making toys for Americans in the unsafe environment could not possibly have afforded those same toys for their own children. This story paints a picture of the disparity between the *haves* and the *have-nots* in our world.[6]

## God's People As Poor People

As we read the minor prophets—and certainly as we study Amos, Hosea, and Micah—we will see that God has a special relationship and covenant with the poor, the abused, the downtrodden, the widow, and the orphan. Jesus, moreover, said that it is very hard for those of us who have a lot of things to enter into the kingdom of God. He compared us to a camel trying to squeeze from tail to snout through the eye of a needle (Matthew 19:24). He also said, "Blessed are you who are poor, for yours is the kingdom of God" (Luke 6:20).

## Implications for Today

Unlike ancient Israel, we must never forget the poor, including the poorly-paid worker. One woman remembers that during her second month at nursing school, the professor gave a pop quiz. This woman said she was a conscientious student and had breezed through the questions until she came to the last one: "What is the first name of the woman who cleans the school?"

*As we read the minor prophets—and certainly as we study Amos, Hosea, and Micah—we will see that God has a special relationship and covenant with the poor, the abused, the downtrodden, the widow, and the orphan.*

Surely this had to be a joke, the woman thought. She remembered that she had seen the cleaning woman several times. She was tall, dark-haired, and in her fifties. *But how would I know her name?* the student wondered. She handed in her paper, leaving the last question blank. Before class ended, one student asked whether the last question would count toward the quiz grade.

"Absolutely," said the professor. "In your careers you will meet many people. All are significant. They deserve your attention and care, even if all you do is smile and say hello."

"I've never forgotten that lesson," said the nurse. "And I learned her name was Dorothy."

"Don't forget Dorothy," Amos said to the Samaritans.

## QUESTIONS

1. How can we as the *haves* relate more genuinely to the *have-nots* of our area, our nation, and our world?

2. Is being rich in and of itself a sin?

3. Should you always charge someone as much as the market will allow? Or, should you always pay someone as little as the market will allow?

4. Why are the poor depicted in Scriptures as having a special place in God's heart?

## NOTES

1. John DeGraaf, Thomas H. Naylor and David Wann, *Affluenza: The All-Consuming Epidemic* (San Francisco: Berrett-Koehler, 2001), 80.
2. See "True World Income Distribution, 1988 and 1993," World Bank Development Research Group, 51–52, at http://econ.worldbank.org/files/978_wps2244.pdf, accessed 1–7–03.
3. Leonard Sweet, *Soul Tsunami* (Grand Rapids: Zondervan, 1999), 334.
4. DeGraaf, *Affluenza*, 36.
5. DeGraaf, *Affluenza*, 24.
6. DeGraaf, *Affluenza*, 77.

## Focal Text

Amos 4:4–5; 5:18–24

## Background

Amos 4:4–13; 5:18–27

## Main Idea

God abhors hypocritical religious ceremonies, calling instead for justice in human relationships.

## Question to Explore

Is worship the most important task of the church?

## Study Aim

To identify ways in which our worship practices may be hypocritical and decide to view them as God does

## Study and Action Emphases

- Affirm the Bible as our authoritative guide for life and ministry
- Develop a growing, vibrant faith
- Value all people as created in the image of God
- Obey and serve Jesus by meeting physical, spiritual, and emotional needs
- Equip people for servant leadership

# LESSON THREE

# Judgment on Religious Hypocrisy

## Quick Read

While the ancient Israelites filled the house of worship with sacrifices and ceremonies, God rejected their worship. God desired righteous living over ritualistic religion.

A seminary professor stated that he had a student who taught in a school for children with hearing disorders in Nashville, Tennessee, for eight years. Although they could hear physically, the children had difficulty understanding what was being said. They could not carry on a logical conversation. The seminary student said, "I just could not stand it any more. I went home crying."

The student said that one year, right after the Thanksgiving holiday, he went to visit a beautiful little girl named Heather. She was seven years old. On the playground, the teacher went over to Heather, took her by the shoulders, positioned himself right in front of her, and asked, "Heather, what did you eat for Thanksgiving?"

Heather replied, "My shoes are red."

"I just couldn't do it anymore," the student told his professor.

The professor said he didn't have the heart to tell the seminarian that he was going to have experiences pretty close to that in church. The professor said he remembered being in Dallas at a church in which the music, the prayers, the sermon, the songs all worked together to create a wonderful worship experience. The professor felt himself in the presence of God. He said, "Standing there after the benediction, I just didn't want to move." There was something about the presence of God in that worship service that immobilized him, and he was just a guest.

A man in the pew in front of the professor, whom the professor did not know, turned around immediately after the worship service and said, "Do you think Tom Landry is going to coach the Cowboys another year?"

"Do you know what that man said to me?" the professor asked. "That man said, 'My shoes are red.'"[1]

The ancient Israelites were focusing on red shoes, too. They were focusing on the wrong thing entirely when it came to worship. They focused on ritual and not righteousness, on giving only their offerings without giving their heart, and on busyness rather than being good to the poor in their community.

## Amos 4:4–5

4 "Enter Bethel and transgress;
  In Gilgal multiply transgression!
  Bring your sacrifices every morning,
  Your tithes every three days.

5 "Offer a thank offering also from that which is leavened,
And proclaim freewill offerings, make them known.
For so you love to do, you sons of Israel,"
Declares the Lord GOD.

# Amos 5:18–24

18 Alas, you who are longing for the day of the LORD,
For what purpose will the day of the LORD be to you?
It will be darkness and not light;
19 As when a man flees from a lion
And a bear meets him,
Or goes home, leans his hand against the wall
And a snake bites him.
20 Will not the day of the LORD be darkness instead of light,
Even gloom with no brightness in it?
21 "I hate, I reject your festivals,
Nor do I delight in your solemn assemblies.
22 "Even though you offer up to Me burnt offerings and your grain
offerings,
I will not accept them;
And I will not even look at the peace offerings of your fatlings.
23 "Take away from Me the noise of your songs;
I will not even listen to the sound of your harps.
24 "But let justice roll down like waters
And righteousness like an ever-flowing stream.

## A Call to Worship (4:4–5)

God's call to worship in this passage was actually sarcastic. His sarcasm is enveloped within a priestly call to worship. The priestly call directed the worshiper to come to the shrine and seek God. King Jeroboam I (931–910 BC) had erected calves at Bethel and Dan so that the people would not travel to the Southern Kingdom, to Jerusalem, to worship (1 Kings 12:26–30). By the time of Amos, during the reign of King Jeroboam II (782–753 BC), these places were popular shrines. Gilgal also was a worship center. In fact, it was the first place in the Promised Land at which Israel had stopped to worship centuries before (Joshua 4:19–24).

God invited the ancient Israelites to go to Bethel and sin and to go to Gilgal and sin some more. He called them to bring all their sacrifices, tithes, and offerings with them when they worshiped. In mimicking style, this call to worship exaggerated the practice of giving. The customary tradition was for families to bring their sacrifices once a year, not every day. Also, the special tithe for the Levites was every third year, not every third day (Deuteronomy 14:22–29). The worshipers of Israel were also gladly giving voluntary freewill and thank offerings in order to impress those around them (Amos 4:5). Amos was cynically suggesting that the ancient Israelites multiply their useless acts of worship—acts that did not please God, who desires justice for the oppressed.

*Each of us should worship God with the realization that ultimately only God's evaluation of us matters.*

Of course, we know from our study in Amos that the Israelites were making their money off the backs of the poor, living self-indulgent lifestyles and selling the souls of the needy for the price of a pair of sandals (2:6; 4:1). Their gifts may have been large, but they were not sacrificial.

The Israelites were not focused on God, on really worshiping God in spirit and in truth. They were focused on themselves.

God knows when we come to worship immersed in ourselves, thinking about other things that occupy our daily lives. God said in essence, *Stop focusing on yourselves, on what you're doing with your offerings, and focus on me. I don't need your sacrifice, but rather the sacrifice of your heart, a heart devoted toward me.*

*We need to seek to understand why God rejected ancient Israel's worship and why God might reject our worship, too.*

To truly worship, you have to stop thinking about yourself. As you focus your heart and mind on God, you'll experience a range of feelings: humility, amazement, awe, mystery, joy, peace, contentment, and fellowship with others also adoring God. When our worship becomes self-conscious, we lose the God-consciousness of worship. If you worship worrying about a myriad of things—things that are going to happen Sunday afternoon or next week—you have failed to focus on God.

## A Warning About God's Judgment (5:18–20)

"The day of the Lord" was a future day in ancient Israel's theology when God would appear to judge the enemies of Israel. The Northern Kingdom was longing for the day of the Lord, the day when they believed they would be put in the position and seat of power. Amos said the day of the Lord would be a day of darkness and despair for ancient Israel, not a day of light and hope. Like a person who escapes a lion only to face a bear, Israel would not escape the day of the Lord no matter how beautiful or spectacular its worship services were.

Each of us should worship God with the realization that ultimately only God's evaluation of us matters. Our self-evaluation, in the end, amounts to nothing. The evaluation of our friends and family has no merit whatsoever. The only evaluation that matters in the final analysis is God's evaluation. As we come to worship, we need to realize we're worshiping the One who ultimately determines our eternal destiny.

*"My shoes are red."*

## A Rejection of Worship (5:21–24)

Amos began to list the elements of the ancient Israelites' worship. As he did so, he stated that God rejected their worship. The Israelites, who surely

# The Day of the Lord

Ancient Israel longed for something called "the day of the Lord." The day of the Lord in the Old Testament was to be a "day of the wrath of the Lord" (Ezekiel 7:19). Sometimes it is called "the great day of the Lord" (Zephaniah 1:14). The idea in the Old Testament portrays a day of dark judgment, including the full coming of the kingdom of God and an end to all the enemies of God.

Israel had viewed the day of the Lord as a day they would welcome. Amos spoiled their hope when he said the day would be a fearful time of judgment for Israel (5:18–20). It would include the destruction of Jerusalem and Israel by foreign powers (2:5; 3:9–11).

In the New Testament, the concept incorporates the final coming of Christ. The Jews were so familiar with the concept of the day of the Lord that sometimes it is simply called "that day" (Matthew 7:22; 1 Thessalonians 5:4; 2 Timothy 4:8) or even simply "the day" (1 Corinthians 3:13).

For the believer, it is a day of joy. For the unbeliever, it is a day of horror (Matt. 10:15; Romans 2:5, 16; 2 Peter 3:7; Revelation 6:17). Much of Paul's writing indicates a longing for the day of the glorious coming of the Christ (2 Corinthians 1:14; Philippians 1:6, 10). (See also John 6:39; Matt. 16:27; 24:30.)[3]

expected praise for their faithful and generous acts of worship, must have been surprised and offended.

Amos pulled no punches in delivering God's message. God declared, "I hate, I reject" your worship services (5:21). In speaking of hating their feasts, Amos was speaking about God's rejection of their celebration of the annual pilgrimage festivals: Unleavened Bread (Passover; Leviticus 23:4–14), Weeks (Pentecost, Lev. 23:15–22), and Tabernacles (Ingathering, Lev. 23:33–44). These feasts represented the occasions when the people of God ordered their lives around the sacred calendar. The Israelites, however, had failed to truly order their lives around God's desire for righteous living.

Amos said that God, furthermore, did not "delight in your solemn assemblies" (5:21). When God appreciated their sacrifice, he breathed in and accepted the sacrifice as a pleasing aroma to his nostrils. Because of the rising odor of the Israelites' sinful lives, including their injustice against the poor, God held his nose when ancient Israel offered a sacrifice. He rejected the odor of their festival worship. Another way of translating Amos 5:21 is, *Nor do I like to smell your solemn assemblies.*

*As worshipers, we have focused an inordinate amount of energy on what kind of music ought to be experienced during a worship service.*

The three sacrifices mentioned next (5:22) are the first three of the five main offerings presented in Leviticus 1—7 (burnt, Lev. 1:1–17; grain, Lev. 2:1–16; peace, Lev. 3:1–17). These three offerings relate most specifically to worship. *I'll have no regard for these*, God said. "I will not accept them" (5:22) is the language of shutting one's eyes. *I won't look on your offerings, much less breathe them in as a sweet aroma*, God said (author's paraphrase of 5:21–22).

Music is the next element of Israelite worship rejected by God (5:23). Look at the body posture of God. God was in heaven above as ancient

# Case Study

When churches try to reach different segments of society with the gospel message, they often change their styles of worship. Many churches offer multiple worship services with each having a different musical style.

Should a church try to provide several styles of worship? What advantages does this approach offer? What challenges surface when a church offers multiple music styles? Are there better solutions?

Israel worshiped. He had shut his nostrils and closed his eyes. Now God had plugged up his ears so he wouldn't even hear the annoying noise they were making in his house of worship.

We need to seek to understand why God rejected ancient Israel's worship and why God might reject our worship, too. Let's explore some reasons God rejected the worship of ancient Israel and why God might reject our worship, too.

First, God rejects our worship when we focus on ritual and religion rather than righteousness (5:21–23). The great oddity of our time is that many churches are splitting up over what we call the "worship wars"—wars about whether we will use the hymn book or sing choruses projected on an overhead screen. We debate over a "contemporary" style versus a "traditional" style. As worshipers, we have focused an inordinate amount of energy on what kind of music ought to be experienced during a worship service.

*The ethics of justice and righteousness are not optional characteristics that would be nice to see in a few worshipers.*

If we consider the mind of God in this passage, we should realize that we are asking the wrong question. In this passage, the style of the music did not cause God to reject the songs of ancient Israel. God did *not* say, *I reject your songs because they're not to the right beat, rhythm, or meter.* What God *did* say in essence is, *I reject your singing and your instrumental pieces because of your heart.*

God hears music completely differently than we do. We might enjoy an accomplished soloist simply for the appeal of the musical presentation. By the time the soloist's music reaches heaven, however, it may sound raspy and rattling to God because the soloist has not come with clean hands and a pure heart, thus lacking righteousness.

On the other hand, there might be a soloist who misses a word and struggles with a musical note here and there, but the heart of the singer is pure and righteous. By the time the struggling song reaches the throne of God, it may be particularly pleasing to the Almighty.

God hears with a different set of ears. When we argue over what type of music to sing, we have missed the point of worship. The question should not be, *To what tune do we sing?* but, rather, *Are our hearts in tune with God when we sing?*

Second, God rejects our worship when we have treated others unfairly (5:24). The ancient Israelites were giving God rivers of religiosity when

God wanted rivers of righteousness and justice. They had been cheating each other all week long, abusing the poor and the needy, and charging for services and goods they had not delivered.

The ethics of justice and righteousness are not optional characteristics that would be nice to see in a few worshipers. The prophet Amos made it clear, without reservation or qualification, that God will reject some worshipers because of their sin.

> *God doesn't look at our rituals. God looks at our heart.*

Nothing is more embarrassing to the church than some of its members conducting themselves in such a way that brings into question their business practices. Folks discover in disgust that they are members of a Baptist church, and the reputation of the community of faith is tainted by their conduct. Our lives in the community, in the classroom, on the coaching field, in the hospital, or on the sales floor must be consistent with what we teach and preach by our presence at worship on Sunday.

## Implications for Today

How do we worship? With clean hands and a pure heart? With a broken spirit and a broken heart over our sin? With sincerity and genuineness?

God doesn't look at our rituals. God looks at our heart. How have we treated others all week long?

One pastor remembers a young woman at a church in Atlanta. She said to the pastor, "This is the first time I was ever in a church."

"Really?"

"Yeah."

"Well," the pastor said, "How was it?"

She said, "Kind of scary."

The pastor said, "Kind of scary?"

She said, "Yeah."

"Why?" the pastor asked.

"It just seems so important," she said. "You know, I never go to anything important. This just seemed so important."[2]

She was right. Worship is just that important—so important it's scary.

## QUESTIONS

1. What kind of worship do you think God enjoys?

2. Is the purpose of worship services primarily to reach people for Christ or to offer adoration to God?

3. How can churches avoid "worship wars"?

4. Why was ancient Israel going to be surprised about "the day of the Lord"? Might we be surprised too?

## NOTES

1. Fred Craddock, *Craddock Stories* (St. Louis: Chalice Press, 2001), 27.
2. Craddock, *Craddock Stories*, 132.
3. H. E. Dosker, "The Day of the Lord," *International Standard Bible Encyclopedia*, vol. 1 (Grand Rapids: Eerdmans, 1979), 879.

## Focal Text

Amos 7:7–17

## Background

Amos 7:1—8:3

## Main Idea

Obeying God is to take precedence over all else.

## Question to Explore

What happens when religion gets cozy with government?

## Study Aim

To identify ways of hearing and obeying God's message in the midst of current culture

## Study and Action Emphases

- Affirm the Bible as our authoritative guide for life and ministry
- Develop a growing, vibrant faith
- Include all God's family in decision-making and service
- Value all people as created in the image of God
- Obey and serve Jesus by meeting physical, spiritual, and emotional needs
- Equip people for servant leadership

# LESSON FOUR God's Message Rejected

## Quick Read

Ancient Israel had gone too far, and God declared that his wrath would be directed at both the places of worship and the kingship of Jeroboam II. Amaziah was little more than a paid-for prophet who tickled the ears of the king. When the church and state are wedded together, preachers lose their prophetic voice.

When I was growing up, I was a sidekick to Leonard Riddle, who was a skilled mason. Laying bricks is a trade of a craftsman. Drive around your town, and you will see many crooked walls slapped up by novices. I was just a teen and never mastered the craft. My job was mixing the mortar and carrying the bricks or the stones to the site for the mason.

Whenever Leonard built a wall, he used a string as his plumb line. The string was his standard of measure. If the wall followed the string, it was straight and strong. If there was space between the string and the wall, then there was something wrong with the wall.

In this Bible study lesson, we will see that there was indeed something wrong with the wall, meaning Israel.

# Amos 7:7–17

7Thus He showed me, and behold, the Lord was standing by a vertical wall with a plumb line in His hand. 8The LORD said to me, "What do you see, Amos?" And I said, "A plumb line." Then the Lord said,

"Behold I am about to put a plumb line
In the midst of My people Israel.
I will spare them no longer.
9 "The high places of Isaac will be desolated
And the sanctuaries of Israel laid waste.
Then I will rise up against the house of Jeroboam with the sword."

10Then Amaziah, the priest of Bethel, sent word to Jeroboam king of Israel, saying, "Amos has conspired against you in the midst of the house of Israel; the land is unable to endure all his words. 11"For thus Amos says, 'Jeroboam will die by the sword and Israel will certainly go from its land into exile.'" 12Then Amaziah said to Amos, "Go, you seer, flee away to the land of Judah and there eat bread and there do your prophesying! 13"But no longer prophesy at Bethel, for it is a sanctuary of the king and a royal residence."

14Then Amos replied to Amaziah, "I am not a prophet, nor am I the son of a prophet; for I am a herdsman and a grower of sycamore figs. 15"But the LORD took me from following the flock and the LORD said to me, 'Go prophesy to My people Israel.' 16"Now hear the word of the LORD: you are saying, 'You shall not prophesy against Israel nor shall you speak against the house of Isaac.' 17"Therefore, thus says the LORD, 'Your wife will become a harlot in the city, your sons and your daughters will fall by the sword, your land will be parceled up by a measuring line and you yourself will die upon unclean soil. Moreover, Israel will certainly go from its land into exile.'"

## Never Again (7:1–9)

The two major sections of Amos are "the words of Amos" found in chapters 1—6 and "the visions of Amos" in chapters 7—9. Our focal text in this lesson concerns the third vision of Amos (7:7–9).

The first vision (7:1–3) is of locusts devouring the crops of Israel. Amos pleaded with the Lord, asking the Lord not to let this take place (7:2). Note what happened: "The Lord changed His mind about this. 'It shall not be,' said the Lord" (7:3). The prayers of one person, Amos, made a big difference. God did not destroy Israel with the plague of locusts.

The second vision, a vision of fire (7:4–6), follows the vision of the devouring locusts. Once again, Amos cried out, saying (author's paraphrase): *Do not do it. Stop, oh Lord. How can Jacob survive?* So the Lord changed his mind a second time (7:6).

In the third vision, our focal text, the Lord asked Amos a question (7;8): "'What do you see, Amos?'" And Amos replied, "'A plumb line'" (7:8). God was saying to Amos, *I am going to be a construction foreman. I am laying a plumb line to see whether my people have measured up to my word. If not, I will spare them no longer* (7:8, author's paraphrase). "My people" is a reference to the covenant Israel had with God. Another way to translate the Hebrew at the end of verse 8 is, *I will never again pass by them,* meaning *I will never again pass over their sins, but, rather, I will pass through their midst.* God's punishment would not be delayed.

*Amaziah was not only a paid-for prophet, but also he was a paid-for prophet by the government.*

God's wrath was directed at both the places of worship and the house of King Jeroboam II (reigned 782–753 BC). The places of worship were to be destroyed. The destruction was to include both the high places, referring to the shrines placed on the hilltops to worship idols, and the established sanctuaries, meaning places of worship like Bethel and Dan that had been placed in the Northern Kingdom as rivals to Jerusalem. The second recipient of God's wrath was going to be the dynasty of Jeroboam II (7:9). God was going to rise up against the house of Jeroboam with the sword.

Notice that this vision, unlike the vision of the locusts and the vision of the fire, has no prayer of intercession, no cry from Amos on behalf of the people. The prophet did not petition God to spare God's people. Amos was silent. This particular vision ended without God changing his mind. The vision ends with the words "no longer" or *never again* trumpeted from the mouth of the prophet and thus from the mouth of God. (A fourth vision appears in 8:1–3.)

Consider these illustrations:

**Illustration 1:** John said to his wife, "Never again will you hurt me like this. I just can't forgive you this time." Ann could feel the pain of his words. His heart was broken, and now he was going to break hers. Never again. No more chances.

> *Each of us has the power to make decisions that change our lives.*

Ann said there was a finality in his words she'd never heard before. She could sense something was different in his voice. Sure, she had hurt him before, and he had hurt her. But despite harsh words, they had never been quite like this. They had always come back together eventually. Never had she heard, "Never again."

She shuttered at the implications of John's verdict. "Never again" sounded so final.

**Illustration 2:** He was shocked beyond belief. The words hit him like nothing had ever hit him before. Despite all the doctor said, he could hear only those words, "You have AIDS."

"Did the doctor say what I thought he said? Surely this is a dream. Surely I'll wake up and there will be no AIDS, there will be no such diagnosis." All he could remember were the words—those three words, "You have AIDS"—every day for the rest of his life. Never again would there be a day, however long he lived, when those words would not haunt him and overshadow everything he did. Never again would he awake to a carefree day with a full life to enjoy. Never again—all because of a stupid, careless

# Thomas Helwys

Many Baptists have suffered in order to secure a church that is free from the state's authority. Englishman Thomas Helwys was an early Baptist who bravely promoted the idea of a church that was separate from the state. He sent King James I, who was the head of both the state and the church, a pamphlet that read:

> [t]he King is a mortal man and not God, therefore [he] hath no power over [the] immortal Soules of his Subjects to make lawes and ordinances for them, and to set Spiritual Lords over them.

Because Helwys questioned the state's right to control religion, he was cast into prison and died there about 1616.[3]

act. He knew there was no one else to blame. The choice had been His. And now life would be "never again."[1] When we hear the words *never again*, the words God uttered to Israel, life changes forever.

We like the first two visions. The first (the locusts are about to devour the sprouting crops when God changed His mind because of the prayer of Amos) brings a sense of hope. The second (the earth is about to be scorched by fire when, once again, God relented) yields relief. I like the picture of God forgiving and forgetting in response to prayers of petition.

But this third scene, the *never again* vision, goes against our image of God providing endless opportunities to repent. God showed Amos a plumb line, a picture from everyday life. God measured his people against his word. God concluded that he would never again change his mind in regard to them. He would never again pass over their sins. The opportunity for holding back God's wrath had passed. The time for intercession was gone. The prophet was silent. The places of worship would be destroyed. The dynasty of Jeroboam would fall—no more chances.

> *When we hear the words* **never again**, *the words God uttered to Israel, life changes forever.*

Amos was a godly man. Prayer really does change the course of events, even when God is involved. The prayers of a righteous person do yield much (James 5:16). Yet, a time came when even the prayer of the prophet could not stop the wrath of God. This time the people of God had crossed the line. God was not going to relent. He was not going to hold back his punishment.

Each of us has the power to make decisions that change our lives. Sometimes our decisions lead us to pain, destruction, and even death. Sometimes our decisions lead us to life, hope, and joy. Pray that you never hear those words *never again*.

## A Paid Prophet (7:10–17)

Expert testimony can be bought for a price. In the courtrooms across America, expert witnesses take the stand every day. As some experts are questioned, they yield answers slanted toward the side that is paying their fee. The expert witness for the defense always seems to have an opinion that clears the client. On the other hand, the prosecution's prophet always seems to bear an opinion that seeks a guilty verdict.

Opinions are bought and sold, bartered and exchanged. Pay enough money and someone will say what you want said. One wonders about the integrity of such practices. An attorney told me that he once cross examined an obstetrician/gynecologist who had spent two hours delivering babies that year and 1400 hours as an expert witness in courtrooms. What was his real profession? Was he a physician or a paid-for prophet? The notion of the paid-for prophet extends far beyond the courtroom. It extends to the pulpits of both ancient Israel and America.

*Every time there is a wedding between the church and the state the offspring are disasters.*

Jim started out with a lot of fervor in his preaching. Jim said what he thought, and he thought what he said. He did not measure his words too carefully because he was just calling it like he saw it. He was declaring, *Thus saith the Lord.* He's not sure when it happened, but, as he looks back over his ministry, he realizes that now he worries more about pleasing the people with his words than he does about pleasing God.

As he "wises up," the preacher begins to lick his finger and test the wind before he hurls any homiletical heat. It's much easier to preach sermons about topics that members want to hear than it is to be faithful to the biblical text. As you look across the billboards of many of America's most popular preachers, you will see sermon titles that sound something like this: "How to Have Success Without Stress," "How to Make Good Marriages Better," or "How to Win at Life."

While certainly appropriate in small doses, that which ought to be the occasional dessert becomes the mainstay. To draw a crowd, theology is reduced to a bare minimum, and people are simply given a baptized version of talk-radio psychology. The focus is on self-help. In due course, this leaves out the majority of the theology of the prophets and apostles. Theology is often tossed aside when we want to fill a building or sell tapes and books.

It's easy to become a paid-for preacher. Maybe that's what happened to Amaziah. He was probably the high priest of Bethel. He was, by all ministerial measures, a soaring success. He was in the big league of pulpits. He was at the "First Church." He had the attention of the king, Jeroboam II. You might say he was a priest at the national cathedral.

Prophets have to be careful that they don't become the spiritual guardian of the status quo, becoming a profiteering puppet who blesses what the king has already decided. In reality, that is what Amaziah had

# Case Study

Do you support teacher-led or coach-led prayer in public schools? As Christians, it is too easy to fall into the trap of pushing our religious beliefs on others using the power of the state. What could possibly be wrong with a public school teacher leading a prayer?

Suppose your family moved to Salt Lake City where your child's public school teacher was reading from the "Mormon Bible" and leading your child in Mormon prayers? Would you still want the state directing your child's spiritual development? How can we build and maintain the wall between the church and the state?

---

become. The more Amaziah ate at the king's table, the more he developed a taste for the king's cuisine. Too, as long as Amaziah kept the king happy, the hors d'oeuvres were going to keep on coming.[2]

About that time, Amos showed up from Judah. Of course, Amos's message was not very popular with the ancient Israelites. He said they were enjoying the prosperity under Jeroboam II mostly because they were breaking the backs of the poor. They were doling out acts of injustice against the marginal people of society.

Amos's radical message didn't sit well with Amaziah, who made his money out of the status quo, out of being the professional prophet to Jeroboam II. Amaziah ratted to the king that Amos was conspiring against him. Amaziah told the king, *Amos is saying that you're going to die and that the rest of us are going into exile* (7:11, author's paraphrase).

*Patriotism and religion must always be distinguishable.*

*Go home*, Amaziah said to Amos. *Go back to your land of Judah*, he seems to be saying. *Eat your bread there and do your prophesying. But no longer prophesy at Bethel, for it is a sanctuary of the king and a royal residence* (7:12, author's paraphrase). Amaziah, the truly paid-for prophet, was accusing Amos of being the same sort of prophet. *Go back and earn your prophetic bread back home in Judah.*

*Wait a minute*, said Amos (7:14–15). *My call to prophecy came from God. God called me to prophesy to Israel, not to Judah. By the way, too, you need to know I'm neither the son of a prophet nor a prophet myself. I'm a herdsman and a fig grower by trade. But God gave me the call. So I've come here to deliver the word* (author's paraphrase).

The words from Amos to Amaziah were harsh: "'Your wife will become a harlot in the city, and your sons and daughters will fall by the sword. Your land will be parceled up by a measuring line, and you yourself will die upon unclean soil. Moreover, all of Israel will go away into exile'" (7:17). All five of these curses on Amaziah were typical results of war.

## God and Country

Amaziah was not only a paid-for prophet, but also he was a paid-for prophet by the government. We must be very careful about baptizing our nation with our religion. Baptists historically have been a people who have declared, *I want my church and my state separate. I can love and serve my country, but that is different from my church. I'm faithful to my country, but I don't want that mixed with my faithfulness to God.*

> Before we get to the point of never again, we need to come to the cross, to the land of beginning again, and partake of the grace of God.

Every time there is a wedding between the church and the state the offspring are disasters. From Constantine to Hitler, those who have joined church and state have produced regretful results. Our Baptist forebears stood, as much as if not more than anybody else, to make sure that America was a free land in which anyone could worship whatever or whomever he or she wanted. We have said the government has no right to tell us how to pray, to whom to pray, or what our pastors should preach. Amaziah, however, had become a paid-for prophet; he had become wedded to the state.

Patriotism and religion must always be distinguishable. When the words "God and country" fit too nicely together in one sentence, you'd better be careful. History has taught us, throughout every nation, that God's people are about to lose when that occurs.

## Implications for Today

When no other people can see the importance of a free church, we as Baptists must build the wall that keeps the church and the state separate. Our pulpiteers, moreover, must have the freedom to utter prophetic words against the sins of our society.

*Never again.* Those are hard words. Before we get to the point of *never again*, we need to come to the cross, to the land of beginning again, and partake of the grace of God.

## QUESTIONS

1.  When does God change his mind? What other examples in Scripture can you think of where God changed his mind?

2.  How can paid ministers keep their preaching prophetically pure?

3.  Why have Baptists historically upheld the separation of the church and the state?

4. What are the dangers of the church receiving a blessing from the state?

## NOTES

1. Illustrations adapted from Cecil P. Staton, Jr., "Never Again," *Interpreting Amos*, ed. Cecil P. Staton, Jr. (Macon: Smyth & Helwys Publishing, 1995), 119–120.
2. Staton, "Never Again," *Interpreting Amos*, 136.
3. Baptist Joint Committee on Public Affairs, *Citizens of Two Kingdoms* (Macon: Smyth & Helwys Publishing, Inc., 1996), 13.

## Focal Text

Amos 9

## Background

Amos 9

## Main Idea

God's judgment on sin is certain, as is the restoration that God offers.

## Question to Explore

What can we count on God to do?

## Study Aim

To decide what I will do about God's message of judgment and restoration

## Study and Action Emphases

- Affirm the Bible as our authoritative guide for life and ministry
- Develop a growing, vibrant faith
- Value all people as created in the image of God
- Equip people for servant leadership

# LESSON FIVE

# Certain Judgment— and Hope

## Quick Read

Amos made clear that there was no place for the ancient Israelites to hide from the judgment of God. Their covenant relationship to God, moreover, should not be presumed upon. The ancient Israelites would be judged just like the people of all nations. Grace, however, was Amos's final word.

Is there any place that we can really hide? Perhaps, once upon a time, there was a place that we might be able to go undetected, a place where we could take cover. Do such places exist anymore? A video camera seems to be mounted in every hallway, at every doorway. But even those video surveillance cameras pale in comparison with what police now have available to them.

One police department boasts that its McDonnell Douglas helicopter is equipped with a thirty-million candlepower searchlight capable of illuminating an entire city block at one time. A Canadian police department, moreover, claims that despite the fact they have had fifteen to twenty calls per shift since their helicopter took to the air a year ago, not a single suspect has ever escaped. From 500 feet away, the infrared camera on the helicopter can pick up a thief's footprints. They appear like heat sources in the snow. When the police pooch loses the scent, the infrared camera keeps following the felon. Watching the infrared camera, the flight crew directs the police on the ground to the suspect. It's not unusual for the flight crew to say, *Officer, he's five feet in front of you. Reach down and touch someone.*

Imagine a law enforcement helicopter this way. You have one and one-half Washington Monuments stacked on top of each other. You stand on top. Add thirty-million candle power. Then throw in infrared sensors that are designed to sense a two-degree difference in heat. From a cruising altitude of 800 feet, police boast you can spot a person without any trouble.

Thus, there is absolutely nowhere to hide, no place to go where the crime choppers on patrol won't find a wrongdoer. So it is in the big cities. So it was for ancient Israel when they tried to escape the wrath, the all-searching eye of God.

Recall that the Book of Amos can be divided into the "words of Amos" in the first six chapters and the "five visions of Amos" in the last three chapters. In chapter 9, we come to the last of the five visions. Last week we looked at the first three visions: the vision of the locusts, the vision of the devouring fire, and the vision of the plumb line. As we move from the first vision to the fifth vision, the role of Amos becomes less dominant, and the Lord takes center stage.

## Amos 9

1 I saw the Lord standing beside the altar, and He said,
"Smite the capitals so that the thresholds will shake,
And break them on the heads of them all!

Then I will slay the rest of them with the sword;
They will not have a fugitive who will flee,
Or a refugee who will escape.

2 "Though they dig into Sheol,
From there will My hand take them;
And though they ascend to heaven,
From there will I bring them down.

3 "Though they hide on the summit of Carmel,
I will search them out and take them from there;
And though they conceal themselves from My sight on the floor of the
    sea,
From there I will command the serpent and it will bite them.

4 "And though they go into captivity before their enemies,
From there I will command the sword that it slay them,
And I will set My eyes against them for evil and not for good."

5 The Lord Gᴏᴅ of hosts,
The One who touches the land so that it melts,
And all those who dwell in it mourn,
And all of it rises up like the Nile
And subsides like the Nile of Egypt;

6 The One who builds His upper chambers in the heavens
And has founded His vaulted dome over the earth,
He who calls for the waters of the sea
And pours them out on the face of the earth,
The Lᴏʀᴅ is His name.

7 "Are you not as the sons of Ethiopia to Me,
O sons of Israel?" declares the Lᴏʀᴅ.
"Have I not brought up Israel from the land of Egypt,
And the Philistines from Caphtor and the Arameans from Kir?

8 "Behold, the eyes of the Lord Gᴏᴅ are on the sinful kingdom,
And I will destroy it from the face of the earth;
Nevertheless, I will not totally destroy the house of Jacob,"
Declares the Lᴏʀᴅ.

9 "For behold, I am commanding,
And I will shake the house of Israel among all nations
As grain is shaken in a sieve,
But not a kernel will fall to the ground.

10 "All the sinners of My people will die by the sword,
Those who say, 'The calamity will not overtake or confront us.'

11 "In that day I will raise up the fallen booth of David,
And wall up its breaches;

I will also raise up its ruins
And rebuild it as in the days of old;
12 That they may possess the remnant of Edom
And all the nations who are called by My name,"
Declares the Lord who does this.
13 "Behold, days are coming," declares the Lord,
"When the plowman will overtake the reaper
And the treader of grapes him who sows seed;
When the mountains will drip sweet wine
And all the hills will be dissolved.
14 "Also I will restore the captivity of My people Israel,
And they will rebuild the ruined cities and live in them;
They will also plant vineyards and drink their wine,
And make gardens and eat their fruit.
15 "I will also plant them on their land,
And they will not again be rooted out from their land
Which I have given them,"
Says the Lord your God.

## Certain Judgment (9:1–8a)

In the first four verses of this section on judgment, we see that there is no hiding place. A whole new emphasis is added to the familiar words, *You can run, but you cannot hide.* The vision begins with Amos observing the Lord standing beside an altar—perhaps the altar of the Bethel shrine, since Amos had preached against the ritualistic religion of that shrine. The altar was the place where God was to receive the offerings given by God's people. Rather than accepting their offerings, the very first word of the Lord is "smite." The passage depicts an earthquake.

The sanctuary that had been used for Israel's sanctimonious services would be completely destroyed. The worship center would tumble like a house of cards. The people would suffer, and, should anyone escape, the Lord would slay them by the sword—that is, by the hand of another nation.

As a matter of comfort, the psalmist (Psalm 139) declared the omnipresence and the omniscience of God.

O Lord, You have searched me and known [me].
You know when I sit down and when I rise up;
You understand my thought from afar.

You scrutinize my path and my lying down,
And are intimately acquainted with all my ways.
Even before there is a word on my tongue,
Behold, O Lord, You know it all.
You have enclosed me behind and before,
And laid Your hand upon me.
[Such] knowledge is too wonderful for me;
It is [too] high, I cannot attain to it.
Where can I go from Your Spirit?
Or where can I flee from Your presence?
If I ascend to heaven, You are there;
If I make my bed in Sheol, behold, You are there.
If I take the wings of the dawn,
If I dwell in the remotest part of the sea,
Even there Your hand will lead me,
And Your right hand will lay hold of me.
If I say, "Surely the darkness will overwhelm me,
And the light around me will be night,"
Even the darkness is not dark to You,
And the night is as bright as the day.
Darkness and light are alike [to You].

Compare the first four verses of Amos 9 with Psalm 139. Both the psalmist and Amos were reflecting a familiar tradition. The psalmist was saying there is nowhere one can go that one is not under the protection of God. Whether it be heaven or Sheol, the abode of the dead, whether it be the sky above or the sea below, *there is no escaping the comforting hand of God*, says the psalmist (author's paraphrase). The psalmist was using all-encompassing language to describe the presence of God.

> *Because God is over both heaven and earth, to try to escape from God is futile indeed.*

Amos was also saying that God is ever present. But instead of saying there is no way to escape God's comfort, Amos was declaring to ancient Israel that there is no place to escape God's wrath. You can run, but you cannot hide.

You can go to the limits of the universe by digging into Sheol or ascending to heaven. But God will find you (9:2). Not only can you not hide in the limits of the universe, you cannot hide in the limits of the earth. God was saying (9:3, author's paraphrase), *It doesn't matter whether you go to the summit of Mount Carmel. I'll pluck you down from there. Or you might try to hide on the floor of the sea. But even there I'll send a serpent to bite you* (see Amos 5:19). God further said, *Though you try to hide among the prisoners of war, the exiles in captivity, I will take the sword of the foreign nation and slay you there* (9:4, author's paraphrase). There are no limits to the pursuit of God.

*. . . Amos was declaring to ancient Israel that there is no place to escape God's wrath.*

This passage in Amos also contrasts with Paul's statement that neither life nor death, nor height nor depth can separate the people of God from the love of God in Christ Jesus (Romans 8:38–39). But just as those in Christ cannot be separated from the love of God, those receiving the wrath of God cannot hide from God either.

One of the most vivid portrayals of the wrath of God comes to us from Jonathan Edwards, who has been described as one of the greatest intellects that America has ever produced. He preached a sermon on July 8, 1741, at Enfield, Connecticut, during the height of revival excitement. The sermon depicted the wrath of God and the heat of hell like no other sermon I've ever read. Tradition says that Jonathan Edwards would simply read the sermon with his face buried in the manuscript. The power of his penned words, however, would cause men and women to grab the pews in front of them until their knuckles turned white.

Edwards said the wrath of God is like a black cloud that hangs directly over our heads, "full of the dreadful storm, and big with thunder; and were it not for the restraining hand of God, it would immediately burst forth upon you." He said further that the wrath of God "is like great waters that are dammed for the present; they increase more and more, and rise higher and higher, till an outlet is given; and the longer the stream is stopped, the more rapid and mighty is its course, when once it is let loose."

*The ancient Israelites thought that being chosen was a privilege when, in fact, it was a responsibility.*

He said that God's wrath is like a bow that is bent. The arrow is aimed at our heart, ready to sting. "And justice bends the arrow at your heart, and strains the bow, and it is nothing but the mere pleasure of God, and that of an angry God, without any promise or obligation at all, that keeps the arrow one moment being made drunk with your blood."

Edwards continued, "Oh sinner! Consider the fearful danger you are in: it is a great furnace of wrath, a wide and bottomless pit. . . ."[1]

# The Church As the People of God

If we insist on a literal interpretation, restoration never took place exactly as depicted in Amos 9. The restoration of God's people takes place in the church. While some try to make a distinction between Israel as the people of God and the church as the people of God, they can do so only by ignoring many teachings in the New Testament.

For example, Paul wrote in Romans 2:28–29, "For he is not a Jew who is one outwardly; neither is circumcision that which is outward in the flesh. But he is a Jew who is one inwardly; and circumcision is that which is of the heart, by the Spirit . . . ." John the Baptist said, "Do not begin to say to yourselves, 'We have Abraham for our father,' for I say to you that God is able from these stones to raise up children to Abraham" (Luke 3:8).

The gathered church—people from every nation who proclaim the Lordship of Christ—is the people of God, the restored Israel (see Galatians 6:16).

---

Verses 5–6 declare: *Don't forget the might of the Lord.* God's power, creativity, and control are presented in this ancient hymn. God is so powerful that he can control the rain or touch the land and cause it to melt. Because God is over both heaven and earth, to try to escape from God is futile indeed.[2]

In verse 7–8a, we see that Israel's covenant status, in the end, was not enough. The ancient Israelites thought that being chosen was a privilege when, in fact, it was a responsibility. Israel had foolishly thought their history with God meant God would always protect them and do good for them. In Amos 3:1–2, though, God said that despite the fact that he had chosen Israel, he was going to punish the nation for its sins.

> *. . . Just as those in Christ cannot be separated from the love of God, those receiving the wrath of God cannot hide from God either.*

Israel was in no way less accountable to God than any of the other nations (9:7). Amos shocked his hearers. He took the very center of their faith experience—God's redemption of their fathers from Egypt—and turned it against them. There is no immunity from God's judgment on sin.

God has been involved with the movements of all the peoples. He said to ancient Israel, *You are like the Ethiopians to me. Or don't forget the Syrians and the Philistines—they had exodus experiences, too* (9:7, author's paraphrase). Did the exodus experiences of the Philistines and the Syrians

# Case Study

Frank's family felt that Frank gave his life to Christ during a youth revival in 1964. He was baptized by the pastor a few weeks after the evangelist left the city. He continued in church while he lived at home, but when he moved away from his family, he also moved away from God. Frank has not shown any interest in the church or in spiritual matters for nearly thirty-five years. Being a Baptist, he has taken confidence in the doctrine of "once saved, always saved." What would Amos say about Frank's spiritual condition? What do you say about Frank's spiritual condition? What do you think God says?

guarantee that they would avoid God's punishment? Of course not. God's eyes were on the sinful kingdom of ancient Israel. The sinful kingdom was equivalent to the leaders of ancient Israel, those involved with the wedding of the church and state: the rich, the priests, the judges, the rulers, and the king. The oppressed, righteous poor, however, were not part of the sinful kingdom.

A wake-up call was issued to ancient Israel. Let it also serve as a wake-up call for the church. Many have comforted themselves with the protection of God based on past religious experiences. Like the ancient Israelites, we cannot afford to look at the good things God has done for us in the past and assume God is still on our side. We cannot look at past experiences and ignore present realities. Living for Christ is not a one-time salvation experience that means we can live as we please beyond our baptism. Rather, we are to take up our cross daily and follow Christ (Matthew 10:38; see also Luke 9:23).

> No scene explains both the wrath and the grace of God better than the cross.

## Certain Hope (9:8b–15)

What seemed like total annihilation is now limited destruction in these verses. The sinful kingdom (Amos 9:8a) and the house of Jacob (9:8b) are not identical. A remnant, a portion of the people, would survive the disaster. The poor and the needy, who were abused and oppressed by the rulers and by the rich, were not condemned. God was going to sift the people. Like grain shaken in the sieve, the house of Israel was going to be shaken among the nations. The grain would be kept, and the chaff would be thrown away (9:9).

Once again, the people thought calamity would not overtake them (9:10). How foolish it is to base our protection, like ancient Israel did, on an event of the past. The Israelites placed their present protection on the past Exodus from Egypt.

God said, however, that he would raise up the fallen house of David (9:11–12). The Davidic dynasty is no longer described as a house (2 Samuel 7:11, 27) but simply as a fallen booth or shelter. Of course, David's restored dynasty was only ultimately fulfilled in the coming of the Christ, the coming of the Messiah who was from the lineage of David and would fulfill the Davidic covenant (Isaiah 9:6–7; 16:5; Jeremiah 23:5; 33:15–17; Ezekiel 34:23–24; 37:24–25; Hosea 3:5; Micah 5:2).

> *Living for Christ is not a one-time salvation experience that means we can live as we please beyond our baptism.*

This new rule of David, this new dynasty, would include a remnant of Edom and the nations. The "people of God" has never included only the people of one nation. Rather, people who fear him from every nation constitute the people of God. In Acts 11, the church realized that even as the Spirit came upon the people of Israel, the Spirit had come upon the house of Cornelius, a Gentile.

Finally, there is a promise of plenty (Amos 9:13–14). *I am going to bless you so much when you find yourself in restoration,* God said. *You are going to plant vineyards and enjoy their produce. You are going to make gardens and eat their fruit* (author's paraphrase). God said that the crop cycle would be so bountiful that before they could completely harvest one crop, they would be plowing for the second one (9:13b).

## Implications for Today

How is it that this passage can include so much about the judgment, the wrath, that comes from God as well as the grace and the restoration of God? No scene explains both the wrath and the grace of God better than the cross. On the cross, God revealed his wrath against his own Son on our behalf. God, by his nature, is holy and righteous. Therefore, God cannot overlook sin. To be true to himself, to be true to his righteousness, God must strike out against sin (Romans 1:18).

How can God be just—that is, righteous—and also the justifier, the one who brings us close to himself? He can only do so for those who have faith in Jesus. Because of the cross, because Jesus' blood has paid for our sins—sins God had previously passed over but could no longer pass over—God is now both just (true to his nature in being righteous) and also the one who justifies or brings us into relationship with himself (Romans 3:26). God's word is a word of punishment. It is also and finally, however, a word of grace.

## QUESTIONS

1. How do you feel and respond when you study biblical passages that present the wrath of God? Are these passages meaningful for contemporary Bible study?

2. Why have Baptists often presumed upon past salvation experiences? How does the idea of "once saved, always saved" relate to passages like Amos 9 that warn against relaxing our relationship with God based upon God's previous blessing?

3. How can God be both wrathful and loving?

4. When is the last time you experienced God's grace?

## NOTES

1. Excerpts taken from Jonathan Edwards, "Sinners in the Hands of an Angry God," Ola Elizabeth Winslow, ed., *Jonathan Edwards: Basic Writings* (New York: The New American Library, 1966), 150–67.
2. Billy K. Smith, *Amos, Obadiah, Jonah*, The New American Commentary (Nashville: Broadman and Holman Publishers, 1995), 158.

# Introducing

## *HOSEA: A God Who Judges and Restores*

What do people think about God's judgment today? Don't they tend to think it's real when it is to be applied to someone else but tend not to think it has much relevance for them? After all, they're good people—good enough, at any rate.

What do people think about God's grace today? This questioning of the reality of God's judgment also means that many tend not to believe they need God's grace. We can handle life just fine ourselves, thank you. Others believe that God's judgment is real but that keeping the rules is all that's important in avoiding it. Since they believe they themselves do that, then if others would just keep the rules, too, there would be no problem. Such attitudes consider grace unnecessary or perhaps even dangerous. Of course, many other people feel so burdened by the difficulties of life that they find it hard to believe that God has a word of grace for them.

The Book of Hosea teaches us that God's judgment and God's grace are both real. Indeed, God's judgment and God's grace are bound together in the Book of Hosea.

Although Hosea is known more for his prophecies of God's merciful promises to restore Israel, judgment actually occupies more than half of the book. As with Amos, Hosea's prophecies are filled with condemnation of his nation for its unfaithfulness to God. Hosea saw this unfaithfulness demonstrated in such things as lawlessness, idolatry, greediness for material gain, oppression of the poor, and reliance on human efforts such as militarism and foreign alliances to solve the people's problems. Such acts disobeyed Israel's covenant with God and were subject to God's judgment.

Even with this emphasis on God's coming judgment, however, the theme that stands out about Hosea is God's gracious promise of restoration. The two prime passages in which this theme is seen are perhaps the best known in the Book of Hosea—(1) Hosea 1—3, in which Hosea's relationship to his wife serves as a metaphor for God's relationship to Israel; and (2) Hosea 11, in which God's love for Israel is couched in terms of a parent's love for a child.

Whatever wrongs Israel had done, God wanted Israel back. Thus, in loving mercy and grace, God offered Israel a way back, the way of repentance. Hosea reminds us that God's grace is both real and available to us if we, too, return to God. Hosea's balance of judgment and grace can help people today who often do not believe in either one.

Hosea prophesied in somewhat the same situation as did Amos. The time period was the middle of the eighth century BC, with the prophecies of Hosea likely coming just a bit later than the prophecies of Amos. In fact, their ministries likely overlapped, although neither mentioned the other. Hosea's prophecies likely relate to the period of time from the mid-eighth century BC into the 720s.

Lesson six, the first lesson on Hosea, is titled "Trouble in the Family." It considers God's message in Hosea's troubled family situation (Hosea 1:1–9). Lesson seven, "Restoring the Relationship," is a study of Hosea 1:10—3:5, and treats God's desire to restore the relationship with Israel in spite of Israel's disobedience. Lesson eight, "God's Charges," provides a summary of God's charges against Israel in Hosea 4—8. Lesson nine, "God's Yearning Heart," focuses on Hosea 11:1–11, in which God expresses loving concern for Israel and promises restoration. Lesson ten, "Return to the Lord," focuses on God's call in Hosea 14 for Israel to repent.[1]

---

Additional Resources for Studying the Book of Hosea:[2]

Roy L. Honeycutt, Jr. "Hosea." *The Broadman Bible Commentary.* Volume 7. Nashville, Tennessee: Broadman Press, 1972.

James Limburg. "Hosea." *Interpretation: A Bible Commentary for Teaching and Preaching.* Atlanta: John Knox Press, 1988.

Jeffrey Rogers. "Hosea." *Mercer Commentary on the Bible.*Volume 4. Macon, Georgia: Mercer University Press, 1996.

Douglas Stuart. "Hosea." *Word Biblical Commentary.* Volume 31. Waco, Texas: Word Books, Publisher, 1987.

Gale A. Yee. "Hosea." *The New Interpreter's Bible.* Volume VII. Nashville: Abingdon Press, 1996.

---

**HOSEA: A GOD WHO JUDGES AND RESTORES**

## NOTES

1.  Unless otherwise indicated, all Scripture quotations in "Introducing Hosea" and the lessons on Hosea are from the New Revised Standard Version Bible, copyright 1989, Division of Christian Education of the National Council of the Churches of Christ in the United States of America. Used by permission. All rights reserved.
2.  Listing a book does not imply full agreement by the writers or BAPTISTWAY PRESS® with all of its comments.

## Focal Text

Hosea 1:1–9

## Background

Hosea 1:1–9

## Main Idea

Unfaithfulness to God leads to rejection by God.

## Question to Explore

Does God really punish sin?

## Study Aim

To summarize how Hosea's family relationships conveyed God's message of judgment to Israel and state implications for life today

## Study and Action Emphases

- Affirm the Bible as our authoritative guide for life and ministry
- Share the gospel with all people
- Develop a growing, vibrant faith

# LESSON SIX

# Trouble in the Family

## Quick Read

In the tragic last days of the Northern Kingdom, God sent the prophet Hosea, whose family served as a living parable of God's unfaithful people.

Everyone in the community told Emily she was making a mistake when she announced her engagement to Joe. Emily would not listen. She entered her wedding plans with complete enthusiasm. She planned in detail a wedding that would be remembered by all who knew them. A few weeks before the wedding, all bridesmaids' dresses had been altered, tuxedos had been reserved, and most other details had been completed.

Then the sky fell on Emily. She caught Joe with another woman, and they were not just having a conversation. What do you think Emily did? What would you do?

If you have ever been betrayed, hurt, or mistreated by someone you love, then you understand Hosea—at least the situation in which he found himself. If someone has ever cheated on you or been unfaithful to you, then you understand Hosea's situation. As you study Hosea, you will better understand how his prophecies reveal God's relationship with the family of God.

## Hosea 1:1–9

¹The word of the LORD that came to Hosea son of Beeri, in the days of Kings Uzziah, Jotham, Ahaz, and Hezekiah of Judah, and in the days of King Jeroboam son of Joash of Israel.

²When the LORD first spoke through Hosea, the LORD said to Hosea, "Go, take for yourself a wife of whoredom and have children of whoredom, for the land commits great whoredom by forsaking the LORD." ³So he went and took Gomer daughter of Diblaim, and she conceived and bore him a son.

⁴And the LORD said to him, "Name him Jezreel; for in a little while I will punish the house of Jehu for the blood of Jezreel, and I will put an end to the kingdom of the house of Israel. ⁵On that day I will break the bow of Israel in the valley of Jezreel."

⁶She conceived again and bore a daughter. Then the LORD said to him, "Name her Lo-ruhamah, for I will no longer have pity on the house of Israel or forgive them. ⁷But I will have pity on the house of Judah, and I will save them by the LORD their God; I will not save them by bow, or by sword, or by war, or by horses, or by horsemen."

⁸When she had weaned Lo-ruhamah, she conceived and bore a son. ⁹Then the LORD said, "Name him Lo-ammi, for you are not my people and I am not your God."

## Background of the Biblical Story

You are always telling your story. What happens in your life will shape your life in one way or another and will be expressed in your words, thoughts, attitudes, choices, and actions. When you are able to see theological connections between your story and the story of the relationship between God and God's people, your story takes on a new dimension.

The story of Hosea is a story of tragedy and love. The story of Hosea reveals the heart of God who desires a loving relationship with the people of God, individually and collectively. On one level, Hosea merely told his own story. On a deeper level, Hosea made theological connections that transcend the centuries.

*If you have ever been betrayed, hurt, or mistreated by someone you love, then you understand Hosea . . . .*

Hosea prophesied during or shortly after the time of Amos. These two were among the first writing prophets. Hosea's message, though, is of a different tone than that of Amos. Whereas the approach of Amos is harsh and blunt, Hosea offered a message of mercy and love. While Hosea's proclamation was less confrontational than that of Amos, Hosea still challenged Israel about the implications of their spiritual unfaithfulness. Amos's message focused more on conduct and outward moral failures. Hosea's message focused more on motives and inward spiritual unfaithfulness. Hosea encouraged the people of God to be faithful to their relationship with God and informs them of the implications of their unfaithfulness.

The Book of Hosea begins by naming the kings who reigned during the tragic last days of the Northern Kingdom (1:1). These tragic years of bloodshed and violence followed centuries of power and prosperity for Israel during the reigns of Saul, David, and Solomon. Following the death of Solomon, the kingdom of twelve tribes had been divided into two nations in 922 BC. During the time of Hosea, Judah to the south was ruled by Uzziah (reigned 783–742 BC), Jotham (reigned 742–735 BC), Ahaz (reigned 735–715 BC), and Hezekiah (reigned 715–687 BC). Israel in the north was ruled by Jeroboam II (reigned 786–746 BC). In the twenty-five years following the death of Jeroboam II, six kings held the throne in Israel. Five of the

*When the people of God live as though the mercy of God is due them, a lack of spiritual commitment is evident.*

six kings reigning over Israel [N.K.] from 746 to 722 BC were assassinated (see 2 Kings 14:29—17:41).

Hosea prophesied for forty to forty-five years, from the middle of the eighth century BC through the fall of Israel in 722 BC. Thus, Hosea is known as the prophet of the decline and fall of the Northern Kingdom. National life in Israel during these years was characterized primarily by moral corruption, social decay, and political lies. Family life had degenerated. The middle class, of pivotal importance in any society, was almost nonexistent. The religious leaders were complacent, guiding people into a religious life that was mainly ceremonial, void of spiritual authenticity. The court system was crooked, and violence was prevalent in the land. Does any of this sound familiar? It was into this context that Hosea offered a compassionate call from a loving, yet just God.

*As you study Hosea, you will better understand how his prophecies reveal God's relationship with the family of God.*

[handwritten marginalia: It's i.e. America & the church of today "O.T."]

## Yahweh's Word (1:1)

The main character in this book is not Hosea. In fact, we barely have any information about him. His name is mentioned only in verses 1–2. Hosea pointed beyond himself to the word of the Lord. The Lord is the main character in this book.

Hosea did not just decide to become a prophet. The word of the Lord (Yahweh) came to him.

When you get your annual physical, the doctor may check your reflexes by taking a small hammer-like instrument and tapping your knee, making your lower leg swing out. Hosea's words are not merely words of wisdom or literary nonfiction. His words came to him as a reflex response to receiving the tap of the word of the Lord.

Here at the beginning of this prophetic book, the expression "the word of the Lord" communicates a significant truth. These words have authority for the readers.

## When Yahweh's Word Intersects Human Living (1:2)

We are not told when God first spoke to Hosea, "'Go, take for yourself a wife of whoredom and have children of whoredom.'" Perhaps God spoke

# Separation of Church and State

On your most recent celebration of Independence Day, you probably heard reminders that centuries of power and prosperity can only continue for America as the nation protects itself against being unfaithful to God. Most of these reminders were well-intended and sincere. Of course, as the church, the people of God in the world, we should always hope, pray, and invest our energies so that people in every nation will be inspired to live faithfully in relationship with God. We must be sure, however, that we do not proclaim the United States to be God's chosen people or wrap the cross of Jesus Christ in the American flag. A historic Baptist principle concerns the separation of church and state. While the church and state influence one another, the wall of separation between them is essential. The church, not the United States of America, is God's chosen people. Furthermore, the church consists of people from every nation and race.

and then Hosea obeyed. Or perhaps Hosea understood the word of the Lord by reflecting theologically on his marriage. What we do know is that Hosea learned significant lessons about himself, the Lord, his family, and his nation by understanding how Yahweh's word intersected his life. For Hosea, Yahweh's word started to intersect his life when he took Gomer to be his wife.

Hosea's marriage to the prostitute, Gomer, was an act of obedience to the Lord. Many students of the Bible offer that Gomer was involved in the cult of Baal. This religion had many shrines throughout Israel. Baal worship involved sexual promiscuity based on the superstition that the fertility of the land depended on the people submitting themselves to the fertility god. Baal worship included shrine prostitutes who availed themselves to the male worshipers as an act of the fertility cult.

*What happens in your life will shape your life in one way or another and will be expressed in your words, thoughts, attitudes, choices, and actions.*

In this drama, Gomer represents Israel. The idea conveyed is that Israel had prostituted herself by worshiping Baal. Hosea represents Yahweh, the legitimate husband. Just as Gomer was unfaithful to Hosea, Israel was unfaithful to Yahweh. Hosea chose Gomer, knowing her inclination toward harlotry, and yet he continued to love her. God chose humanity, knowing our inclination toward unfaithfulness, and yet God continues to love us.

Israel did not worship Baal alone. Israel worshiped several gods and perceived Yahweh to be one of the gods to be worshiped. This practice was, of course, in direct disobedience to the commandments of God in the law of Moses (Exodus 20:3–4).

The same commandments given to the people of God through Moses and emphasized through Hosea continue to be commandments for the people of God today. God is not to be *one* of the gods we worship. God is to be the *only* One we worship. In a time when a desire for spirituality is widely acclaimed as being on the increase, it is essential to remember that our thirst must be for God, not for spirituality. Focusing on spirituality can meet the requirements of being in style with the movement of society. But only focusing on the one true and living God meets the requirements of being in step with the Spirit. It is possible to study and know much about theology and theologians and theologies, yet still not know *Theo* (form of the Greek word for *God*).

> The story of Hosea reveals the heart of God who desires a loving relationship with the people of God, individually and collectively.

Before we begin to denounce the practices and lifestyles of the rich and famous, the entertainment, the media, and the superstars of music and sports, let us look at ourselves. Are you focused on God? Do you dabble in your horoscope? Do you pay attention to your fortune cookie? Are you superstitious? Exodus 20:3–4 is for you too.

Listening to your life is important. This is one way to get to know your self from the inside out. As you take the time to ask how your life and your relationship with your family reveal something to you about the heart and character of God, you will experience a deeper understanding of how the word of the Lord intersects your life.

## When People Become More than Living Symbols (1:2–9)

Hosea's marriage to Gomer and the three children that were born by Gomer are symbolic, but they are more than symbols. They are representations of the relationship between God and God's people.

A mother once was describing her children. *One of my children*, she said, *is always finding the line of right versus wrong and exploring just beyond the border of right. This child is a challenge for me*, she continued, *because through this child I am confronted with my own interests in what lies beyond the borders of righteous living. One of our other children is deeply committed to the ways of the Lord related to morality and sets high expectations for friends to have the same*

74

*level of commitment. This results in only a limited number of friends. Through this child, I am confronted with my own inclination toward being judgmental and narrow-minded toward those who do not agree with my perspectives or follow my moral compass. Our other child is able to live from a spiritually authentic heart, always tender and giving, and is ever willing to give time and self to someone in need. Yet this same child can also be angry and lazy. Through this child, I am confronted with the gaps between what is possible in me and what earthbound characteristics conflict against my spiritual nature.* This mother has discovered that her children are more than living symbols; they are representations of her relationship with God.

*While Hosea's proclamation was less confrontational than that of Amos, Hosea still challenged Israel about the implications of their spiritual unfaithfulness.*

The three children birthed by Gomer were results of her unfaithfulness (1:2). Hosea heard the word of the Lord telling him to give a specific name to each child. Each name represented an implication of judgment against Israel for her unfaithfulness to Yahweh.

The first result of unfaithfulness was a child named Jezreel. Yahweh instructed Hosea to name him Jezreel. Jezreel was about halfway between the Sea of Galilee and Samaria and thus in the northern half of Israel. Second Kings 9—10 tells of the day when Jehu was anointed to be king and instructed to avenge the Lord against Ahab and Jezebel. This incident occurred about a hundred years prior to the time of Hosea. Ahab and Jezebel had introduced Israel to Baal worship. Jezreel was the location where Jezebel had killed Naboth to seize his vineyard (see 1 Kings 21). Jezreel became the location of Jezebel's death. But, rather than seeking the will of the Lord, Jehu became violent and took matters into his own hands. The result was that the Lord now sought to punish the house of Jehu for his massacre at Jezreel. This first child was named Jezreel to warn Israel that because of their unfaithfulness, there would be repercussions for them to pay.

*Anyone unfaithful to God by following pursuits other than the will of God will experience the rejection of God.*

In American society, distractions and attractions are everywhere, enticing people away from faithfulness to God. Yet it is essential to remember that God is aware of unfaithfulness. A person may forget spiritual unfaithfulness, but God will remember. The birth of Jezreel is a reminder to God's people today that there are repercussions to spiritual infidelity. Anyone

# Spirituality

A congregation has found itself reaching people in its community with new-found effectiveness. There is a problem, however. Many of these people desire a new depth in spirituality—in general. The spirituality they are interested in is concerned more with feeling good than with being faithful or fulfilling ethical demands. Their interest in the lordship of Jesus Christ and the authority of Scripture is minimal. They are seeking a religious life that embraces several religious traditions with the Christian perspective holding a highly honored position. What suggestions do you have for this congregation as they seek to make disciples in their community?

unfaithful to God by following pursuits other than the will of God will experience the rejection of God.

A second child, Lo-ruhamah, was born through Gomer's unfaithfulness. "Ruhamah," in Hebrew, means *pity* or *mercy*. But the prefix, "lo," means *no* or *not*. Therefore, Lo-ruhamah means *no mercy* or *not pitied*. Due to Israel's unfaithfulness, God withdrew from expressing mercy to them.

Mercy should never be expected. Mercy is a gift due to the compassion involved in the relationship. When the people of God live as though the mercy of God is due them, a lack of spiritual commitment is evident.

The third result of unfaithfulness was a child named Lo-ammi. In Hebrew, "Ammi" means *my people*. This term is taken from the covenant relationship between God and Israel. As Hosea continued to prophesy, the people of God continued to be unfaithful. Thus, God disowned Israel by saying, "You are not my people" (1:10).

As you look backwards in your theological rearview mirror, you see this story through the lens of Jesus Christ. Surely the life and teachings of Christ reveal God to us as one who will never withdraw mercy. Too, even if God were to withdraw mercy, it would seem to occur only when a person has truly been evil. But here in the prophecy of Hosea, God withdraws mercy when unfaithfulness is evident. Too, lest we forget, Jesus gave several warnings related to impending desolation and judgment. Not all of Jesus' words were sweet like honey.

> As you take the time to ask how your life and your relationship with your family reveal something to you about the heart and character of God, you will experience a deeper understanding of how the word of the Lord intersects your life.

## Implications for Today

For Hosea, his family and his calling were interwoven. He understood the heartache of God for Israel because he experienced heartache through Gomer's unfaithfulness. When there is trouble in the family, every member of the family should become active in solving the problems. When the family of God is being unfaithful to God, the heart of God is in pain.

The word of the Lord as revealed through Hosea reminds us that God has the last word. Where there is unfaithfulness, God pronounces judgment.

Are you being attentive to the principles of the Lord? Do you realize the need to repent from unfaithfulness and seek the Lord? Remember, you are always telling your story, but God has the last word. God is always at work where there is trouble in the family.

## QUESTIONS

1. List and describe the feelings that are present when someone is unfaithful to you. How does this list assist you in understanding how God feels toward the unfaithful people of God?

2. Why do you think prosperity seems to foster a lack of responsibility?

3. How would you propose to help people understand the justice of God through a loving and relational perspective?

4. What words come to mind in contrasting the prophecies of Amos and Hosea? Which approach—Hosea's or Amos's—is most appealing to you? Why?

5. In what ways do American Christians try to combine worshiping the Lord and worshiping other gods? What other gods compete with the Lord for the faithfulness of God's people?

6. Do you believe God would ever withdraw mercy from the church because of unfaithfulness, or does this conflict with the revelation of God we are given in Jesus Christ?

## Focal Text

Hosea 1:10—2:5, 14–23; 3:1–5

## Background

Hosea 1:10—3:5

## Main Idea

God takes action to restore people who have gone away from him.

## Question to Explore

How does God respond to us when we have sinned?

## Study Aim

To draw implications for how God wishes to relate to us from what the passage teaches about the relationship God desired with Israel

## Study and Action Emphases

- Affirm the Bible as our authoritative guide for life and ministry
- Share the gospel with all people
- Develop a growing, vibrant faith
- Value all people as created in the image of God

# LESSON SEVEN Restoring the Relationship

## Quick Read

Sin is not merely the violation of divine laws and rules; sin is the violation of a relationship that God seeks to restore.

A tragedy occurred in the life of George Truett when he was on a hunting trip with some other men, early in his ministry as pastor of First Baptist Church, Dallas, Texas. At the end of a day of hunting, Truett's gun accidentally discharged. A load of buckshot struck one of his fellow hunters in the leg. The man was J. C. Arnold, chief of police for Dallas and a friend of Truett's. The wound itself did not seem serious, but Arnold died five days later from complications.

Truett was heartbroken. He believed his carelessness had led to the death of a friend.

After Arnold's death, Truett was deeply troubled. He did not sleep for a week. He told his wife he would never preach again. After finally falling asleep at last one night, Truett dreamed that Jesus appeared to him with a word of encouragement. Word spread through the community that Truett would preach on the following Sunday morning. A person who was there that day said:

> His face was drawn, and his eyes were so sad. When he stood to preach, he remained silent for a long moment. You could have heard a pin drop. When he began, somehow he sounded different. His voice! I shall never forget his voice that morning, as we heard for the first time the note of sadness and pathos which later we came to know so well. It seemed to carry the burden of all the grief in the world.

Truett served as pastor of First Baptist, Dallas, for forty-five years after that terrible, life-changing experience in 1898. His experience of grief and sorrow shaped his spirit so that he was forever more sensitive to those who were in trouble, hurting, suffering, and heartbroken.[1]

God is in the business of restoration. Whether the cause of personal anguish is by accident or by disobedience, God takes the initiative in the mission of mending broken lives, healing hurts, ministering to the suffering, and rescuing those who are in trouble. In addition, God calls a people to partner in this mission.

# Hosea 1:10–11

[10]Yet the number of the people of Israel shall be like the sand of the sea, which can be neither measured nor numbered; and in the place

where it was said to them, "You are not my people," it shall be said to them, "Children of the living God."[11]The people of Judah and the people of Israel shall be gathered together, and they shall appoint for themselves one head; and they shall take possession of the land, for great shall be the day of Jezreel.

# Hosea 2:1–5, 14–23

[1]Say to your brother, Ammi, and to your sister, Ruhamah.

2  Plead with your mother, plead—
    for she is not my wife,
    and I am not her husband—
    that she put away her whoring from her face,
    and her adultery from between her breasts,

3  or I will strip her naked
    and expose her as in the day she was born,
    and make her like a wilderness,
    and turn her into a parched land,
    and kill her with thirst.

4  Upon her children also I will have no pity,
    because they are children of whoredom.

5  For their mother has played the whore;
    she who conceived them has acted shamefully.
    For she said, "I will go after my lovers;
    they give me my bread and my water,
    my wool and my flax, my oil and my drink."

· · · · · · · · · · · · · · · · · · · · · · · · · · · · · · · · · · · · · · · · · · · · · · · · · · · · · · · · · · · · · · · · · · · · · ·

14  Therefore, I will now allure her,
    and bring her into the wilderness,
    and speak tenderly to her.

15  From there I will give her her vineyards,
    and make the Valley of Achor a door of hope.
    There she shall respond as in the days of her youth,
    as at the time when she came out of the land of Egypt.

[16]On that day, says the LORD, you will call me, "My husband," and no longer will you call me, "My Baal." [17]For I will remove the names of the Baals from her mouth, and they shall be mentioned by name no more. [18]I will make for you a covenant on that day with the wild animals, the birds of the air, and the creeping things of the ground; and I will abolish the bow, the sword, and war from the land; and I will make you lie down in safety. [19]And I will take you for my wife forever; I will take you for my wife

in righteousness and in justice, in steadfast love, and in mercy. <sup>20</sup>I will take
you for my wife in faithfulness; and you shall know the LORD.

<sup>21</sup> On that day I will answer, says the LORD,
I will answer the heavens
and they shall answer the earth;
<sup>22</sup> and the earth shall answer the grain, the wine, and the oil,
and they shall answer Jezreel;
<sup>23</sup> and I will sow him for myself in the land.
And I will have pity on Lo-ruhamah,
and I will say to Lo-ammi, "You are my people";
and he shall say, "You are my God."

## Hosea 3:1–5

<sup>1</sup>The LORD said to me again, "Go, love a woman who has a lover and is
an adulteress, just as the LORD loves the people of Israel, though they turn
to other gods and love raisin cakes." <sup>2</sup>So I bought her for fifteen shekels of
silver and a homer of barley and a measure of wine. <sup>3</sup>And I said to her,
"You must remain as mine for many days; you shall not play the whore,
you shall not have intercourse with a man, nor I with you." <sup>4</sup>For the
Israelites shall remain many days without king or prince, without sacrifice
or pillar, without ephod or teraphim. <sup>5</sup>Afterward the Israelites shall return
and seek the LORD their God, and David their king; they shall come in awe
to the LORD and to his goodness in the latter days.

### The Living God Turns Reality Downside Up (1:10—2:1)

After having proclaimed Jezreel, Lo-ruhamah, and Lo-ammi to be results
of unfaithfulness in Hosea 1:1–9, God overturned these pronouncements.
In Hosea 1:10–11, the word of the Lord
refers to Jezreel as a great day rather than a
day of judgment. In the very place where the
people of God were called Lo-ruhamah, "not
my people," they were to be called, "Children
of the living God" (1:10). In 2:1, the names are inverted in sequence and
pronounced Ammi and Ruhamah—*pitied* and *my people*, respectively.

> The living God turns
> reality downside up.

God turned reality downside up. This is God's nature. No matter
how terrible the degree of unfaithfulness, God desires to restore the
relationship.

The many gods of Baal worship were mere idols, not living deities. Idols can take no initiative, but the living God takes initiative toward wayward children. Non-living idols can receive allegiance from submissive worshipers, but only a living God can restore a relationship that has been broken.

Today, individuals may express loyalty to many possessions, priorities, pursuits, principles and privileges. There continues, however, to be only one true and living God with whom people may have a relationship. This relationship can exist only because of the initiative of the Lord. When God takes this initiative, the very places in life that were desolate are filled with joy. The living God turns reality downside up.

## The Agony of Victory (2:2–5)

For many years, the phrase heard across America on Saturday afternoons, via a television sports show, "The Wide World of Sports," was, "The thrill of victory; the agony of defeat." If, however, a victory is truly worth the struggle, there will be agony involved. The most important victories of life require the agony of a struggle.

Hosea held forth hope to the children of Gomer, proclaiming that the Lord held forth hope to the children of Israel. Hosea desired Gomer, and the Lord desired Israel. "Plead with your mother, plead," said Hosea to the children of Gomer. There is agony in his challenging words. The relationship was a struggle for the loving husband, Hosea. He asked for the help of the children.

> *The most important victories of life require the agony of a struggle.*

As Hosea desired Gomer, the Lord desired Israel. Requirements needed to be met, however, if the relationship was to be restored. The unfaithfulness must cease. The pursuit of other gods must end. Otherwise, if the unfaithfulness continued, there would be public embarrassment, loneliness, and a lack of fulfillment. Hosea 2:6–13 tells of actions that God would take to discipline Israel to return and be faithful to him.

The lifestyle of sinful living is gratifying and exciting. If it were not, people would avoid it. But the fun that results from living outside the will of the Lord is short-lived and mixed with purposelessness, emptiness, and misery.

For the person who has been unfaithful to God, there may be agony in confession of and repentance from sinful living. Still, the ownership of personal responsibility is essential to the relationship being restored. The

Lord always desires for the relationship to be restored but requires humility and vulnerability of spirit. There may be agony along the journey to victory, but the agony is worth the cost for the victory to be known.

## Hidden in Plain Sight (2:14–23)

Sometimes the most difficult person to forgive is oneself. In the introductory story for this lesson, George Truett had to move past his sense of failure and sorrow to embrace the embrace of God. He had to accept his *acceptedness.* He had to forgive himself. He had to come to the place where he sensed he was worthy of being useful again. Before he could be restored in his relationship with God's will for his life, George Truett needed to reach a point of readiness by hearing a word of encouragement.

> Sometimes the most difficult person to forgive is oneself.

Even before there is a realization that God is at work, the Lord takes initiative on behalf of God's people. As the Lord began to work at restoring a relationship of faithfulness with Israel, the Lord said, "I will now allure her . . . and speak tenderly to her" (2:14). In order to restore the relationship, the Lord began to court the estranged people of God.

Even while a person is wandering in the despair of sin, trouble, suffering, or sorrow, the Lord is whispering sweet, encouraging words. The Lord is seeking to nurture a response that restores the relationship of love.

Eventually, on the day of recommitment, the beloved would refer to the Lord as, "My husband" (2:16). The unfaithful would be restored to a relationship of fidelity (2:17). A renewal of the covenant would bring peace where there had been strife, safety where there had been enmity (2:18). Righteousness, justice, love, mercy, and faithfulness (2:19–23) would characterize the restored relationship.

Even today, in your life and in the lives of those you love, the Lord is at work, hidden in plain sight.

## A Love That Will Not Stop (3:1–2)

Reading through the Book of Hosea offers challenges for the reader. How or whether the book is organized chronologically or sequentially is not as

# Worship of Baal

The word *baal* traces back to a word meaning *lord, husband, owner,* or *master.* Some documents dating back to the fifteenth century BC describe Baal to be a storm or weather god. Baal was believed to be the god who brought rain and thus was understood to be a fertility god.

The worship of Baal was practiced in Palestine during the years of Hebrew settlement, following the Exodus from Egypt and the wilderness wanderings. On entering the Promised Land, the Hebrew people often embraced the worship of Baal that had been practiced by the Canaanites before them.

During the reign of Ahab in the Northern Kingdom (reigned 869–850 BC), Baal worship grew in popularity due to the influence of Jezebel. During these years, many Baal missionaries were sent out, and temples for Baal were constructed.

Baal worship included temple prostitution. The prophets who condemned Baal worship most profoundly were Elijah, Elisha, Jeremiah, and Hosea.

---

clear as we might like. What the reader is told in 3:1 is that the word of the Lord came to Hosea again. The reader is not told the lapse of time between chapters 1 and 3. This time, the message was for Hosea to continue initiating love toward Gomer despite all that had happened. God instructed Hosea to buy her out of slavery. Evidently, through her years of harlotry, Gomer had lost her beauty and her charm. At some point she may have sold herself into slavery simply to survive. The message offered here is that God's love will never stop pursuing the beloved.

There is a pronounced difference between love that is motivated by the human will and love motivated by God's will. Human love is expressed when someone is deemed to be lovable due to the person's appearance or value to the lover. The human being, created in the image of God, needs to express love. Therefore, a person is willing to express human love when someone is pleasing to the senses. On the other hand, love motivated by the will of God

*Even today, in your life and in the lives of those you love, the Lord is at work, hidden in plain sight.*

is expressed in spite of the lack of such qualities and even due to the need of the one receiving love. Love that is motivated by the will of God can only be expressed by a person or a community of individuals when differences, limitations, faults, and imperfections are placed in the background and needs are placed in the foreground.

For Hosea to express love for Gomer after years of unfaithfulness, after she had lost her attractiveness and while she was living in bondage, he would need a motive beyond human love to be at work in his life. Thus, once again, the word of the Lord came to him. Hosea was open to the word of the Lord. Because he was open to the word of the Lord, Hosea was able to look beyond Gomer's sin, beyond her faults, and beyond her ugliness to see her need to be loved. If he had not first been willing to be motivated by the love of God, he would never have been willing to pay a price on her behalf.

*You are saved from sin to a relationship with God through Christ for ministry through the mission of God in your daily life.*

Hosea 3 is a picture of redemption. The idea communicated is that of the Lord paying a price to buy back someone who already belongs to the Lord. In this passage, the Christian reader is able to see similarities between the story of Hosea and the story of Jesus, the Christ. The concept of divine suffering is present. The initiative of grace is clear. The need for costly love is revealed. The purchase out of slavery to sin is evident. This brief chapter reminds the reader of Paul's words to the church in Rome: "God proves his love for us in that while we still were sinners Christ died for us" (Romans 5:8).

But why was Gomer purchased back? Was there to be a purpose in her life? She was saved from slavery to a relationship, but why?

## Saved From, To, and For (3:3–5)

Many Christians have never understood why they have been saved from sin to a relationship with God through Jesus Christ. Some mistakenly believe that it is for the purpose of being good members of the institutional church— paying their tithes, belonging to a congregation in order to get help raising the kids so that they too may become good church members, and on and on and on. Some others mistakenly believe that it is for the purpose of having the correct doctrinal or theological perspective—saying the right words, pledging allegiance to the correct written documents, etc. Still others mistakenly believe that they have been

*We have been saved, bought with a great price, for the purpose of becoming involved with God on mission.*

86

saved for the purpose of arguing about social issues, defending ethical positions in a political manner, etc.

Every Christian has a purpose far greater than any of these purposes. Every Christian is to be on mission with God in continuing the ministry of Jesus Christ. You are saved *from* sin *to* a relationship with God through Christ *for* ministry through the mission of God in your daily life.

*Whether the cause of personal anguish is by accident or by disobedience, God takes the initiative in the mission of mending broken lives, healing hurts, ministering to the suffering, and rescuing those who are in trouble.*

Just as Gomer needed to experience a transformation in lifestyle (3:3), Israel needed to be transformed as well (3:4–5). Israel needed to go through a period of time without national order, public worship, or private worship. Sacrifice was an act of worship. A pillar was a symbol of divine presence. It was a stone placed on a worship site. Ephod and teraphim represented private expressions of spirituality based on superstition. An ephod was used to find the divine will for the future. A teraphim was a small graven image used in ancestor worship. Israel needed a transformation in lifestyle.

If the relationship between God and any person is to be restored, there must be a transformation in lifestyle. We cannot live as followers of the One who paid the price to purchase us out of the bondage of slavery without having a transformation in our lifestyle. We must be willing to be still and listen for the word of the Lord. We must seek to discern and follow the will of God.

We have been saved, bought with a great price, for the purpose of becoming involved with God on mission. The restoration of our relationship with God calls us to refocus and reorder the way we live.

## More Implications for Today

The most difficult question you will ever face is this: _Do you have the will to will God's will in your life?_ As one of the people of God, a member of the body of Christ, the church, you have been given the responsibility of being involved in the mission of God. At some point in your life, you realized you were like Gomer, in need of redemption. You desired a restored relationship with God. You had pursued images, non-living deities, and

# Getting a Missional Perspective

Use the following checklist to identify ways you or your class might be a catalyst to help people move from an institutional, doctrinal, or ethical perspective to a missional perspective on the Christian life.

## Institutional

- From paying tithes to being faithful stewards of missional resources
- From belonging to a congregation to implementing missional initiatives

## Doctrinal

- From having the correct theological perspective to engaging in missional partnerships
- From pledging allegiance to written documents to living out missional theology

## Ethical

- From debating social issues to being involved on behalf of the disenfranchised
- From defending ethical positions in a political manner to engaging in ministry in daily life

---

selfish involvements based on your human senses. Then you accepted the price that was paid on your behalf and your life changed. You became a recipient of God's mercy. You became one of the people of God.

*The most difficult question you will ever face is this: Do you have the will to will God's will in your life?*

Now, day by day by day you are challenged to have the will to will God's will in your life. Each day, you are challenged to open your life to the word of the Lord, Jesus Christ, the Word made flesh. Each day, you are called, equipped, and commissioned to be involved in the mission of God, expressing divinely motivated love to people because of their need to be loved. You are now a partner with the Lord in restoring the relationship between God and humanity.

## QUESTIONS

1. How can living through personal anguish, whether caused by accident or disobedience, make a person more sensitive to the needs of others?

2. How has God has turned your world downside up? How did you know it was God and not just circumstantial timing?

3. What if the life of faithfulness to the Lord were easier and more exciting to the human senses? Why do you think God created faithfulness so that it is connected to sacrifice, humility, and obedience?

4. Do you think there are ever reasons a relationship is not worth making the effort to seek restoration?

5. Have there been occasions when you realized God was hidden in plain sight working on your behalf or on behalf of someone you love, nurturing you or your loved one back into a faithful spirit-to-Spirit relationship?

6. How do the characteristics of love motivated by the human senses and love motivated by the will of God contrast and compare? (See 1 Corinthians 13 for some clues.)

## NOTES

1. C. Douglas Weaver, ed., *From Our Christian Heritage* (Macon, Georgia: Smyth & Helwys Publishing, Inc., 1997), 363-364, citing Leon McBeth, *The First Baptist Church of Dallas* (Grand Rapids: Zondervan Publishing House, 1968), 136-138, for the quotation.

## Focal Text

Hosea 4:1–12; 8:1–10, 14

## Background

Hosea 4—8

## Main Idea

Religious beliefs and practices can transform a society for the good or lead it into evil.

## Question to Explore

How should faithfulness to God be demonstrated in our day?

## Study Aim

To describe parallels between our practices and God's charges against Israel and identify implications for action

## Study and Action Emphases

- Affirm the Bible as our authoritative guide for life and ministry
- Develop a growing, vibrant faith
- Obey and serve Jesus by meeting physical, spiritual, and emotional needs
- Equip people for servant leadership

# LESSON EIGHT

# God's Charges

## Quick Read

God's charges against the people of God in Hosea's day are relevant for today's church. Since religious sincerity can transform a society for good or evil, what can we do?

The setting is a courtroom. No, it is not a television show set for *The Practice*, *Law and Order*, *People's Court*, or *Family Law*. This is serious. This is real. This is the case of *The Lord vs. the People of God*.

You can pretend as though this is just a story, of course. You can look at Hosea 4—8 as if it were fictional literature or another episode out of an ancient history book if you like. This case, though, is about you. Charges are being brought against you, and the One sitting in the witness chair is not pointing at your pastor or staff, or everyone in your class, your congregation, your denomination, or the church around the world. The One sitting in the witness chair is pointing directly at you and stating these words of indictment:

> There is no faithfulness or loyalty, and no knowledge of God in the land. Swearing, lying, and murder, and stealing and adultery break out; bloodshed follows bloodshed. Therefore the land mourns, and all who live in it languish; together with the wild animals and the birds of the air, even the fish of the sea are perishing. . . . My people are destroyed for lack of knowledge. . . . And since you have forgotten the law of your God, I will also forget your children (Hosea 4:1b–3, 6).

## Hosea 4:1–12

1 Hear the word of the LORD, O people of Israel;
for the LORD has an indictment against the inhabitants of the land.
There is no faithfulness or loyalty,
and no knowledge of God in the land.
2 Swearing, lying, and murder,
and stealing and adultery break out;
bloodshed follows bloodshed.
3 Therefore the land mourns,
and all who live in it languish;
together with the wild animals
and the birds of the air,
even the fish of the sea are perishing.
4 Yet let no one contend,
and let none accuse,
for with you is my contention, O priest.
5 You shall stumble by day;
the prophet also shall stumble with you by night,
and I will destroy your mother.

6 My people are destroyed for lack of knowledge;
   because you have rejected knowledge,
   I reject you from being a priest to me.
   And since you have forgotten the law of your God,
   I also will forget your children.
7 The more they increased,
   the more they sinned against me;
   they changed their glory into shame.
8 They feed on the sin of my people;
   they are greedy for their iniquity.
9 And it shall be like people, like priest;
   I will punish them for their ways,
   and repay them for their deeds.
10 They shall eat, but not be satisfied;
   they shall play the whore, but not multiply;
   because they have forsaken the Lord
   to devote themselves to 11whoredom.
   Wine and new wine
   take away the understanding.
12 My people consult a piece of wood,
   and their divining rod gives them oracles.
   For a spirit of whoredom has led them astray,
   and they have played the whore, forsaking their God.

# Hosea 8:1–10, 14

1 Set the trumpet to your lips!
   One like a vulture is over the house of the Lord,
   because they have broken my covenant,
   and transgressed my law.
2 Israel cries to me,
   "My God, we—Israel—know you!"
3 Israel has spurned the good;
   the enemy shall pursue him.
4 They made kings, but not through me;
   they set up princes, but without my knowledge.
   With their silver and gold they made idols
   for their own destruction.
5 Your calf is rejected, O Samaria.
   My anger burns against them.
   How long will they be incapable of innocence?
6 For it is from Israel,

an artisan made it;
it is not God.
The calf of Samaria
shall be broken to pieces.
7 For they sow the wind,
and they shall reap the whirlwind.
The standing grain has no heads,
it shall yield no meal;
if it were to yield,
foreigners would devour it.
8 Israel is swallowed up;
now they are among the nations
as a useless vessel.
9 For they have gone up to Assyria,
a wild ass wandering alone;
Ephraim has bargained for lovers.
10 Though they bargain with the nations,
I will now gather them up.
They shall soon writhe
under the burden of kings and princes.

14 Israel has forgotten his Maker,
and built palaces;
and Judah has multiplied fortified cities;
but I will send a fire upon his cities,
and it shall devour his strongholds.

## When God Complains (4:1–12)

Having been raised in parsonages and having ministered in congregational settings for more than twenty-five years, I have grown a third ear listening to people's complaints. The comments go like this: "It was too hot in the sanctuary." "It was too cold in the sanctuary." "We sang that hymn too slow." "The youth minister's pants are too tight." "The Wednesday night menu is too starchy." This is just a sample of the many complaints that consume the energy and attention of the Holy Spirit empowered, missional people of God. Does it surprise you that the church across America is on the decline?

How, though, do we develop a discerning ear to listen to the complaints of God? If you're anything like me, you do not want to sound over-reactive like one of those people in the news all of the time—you know, the "Chicken Littles," the ones who suggest that every little issue is some kind of attack by Satan or punishment from God.

Somehow, Hosea was able to hear the complaints of God in his day. When you listen closely to the complaints from almost three thousand years ago, it sounds quite similar to some things people talk about today. Since God is the same yesterday, today, and forevermore, maybe we should pay close attention to these complaints and figure out what we need to be doing to remedy these situations in our own lifetime.

No doubt, Hosea was a creative person. In the first three chapters, we have been introduced to his marriage and family. With creative imagination, Hosea heard the word of the Lord revealed through his experience of having an unfaithful wife and children born by way of prostitution. Hosea was able to prophesy and proclaim the word of the Lord to Israel by understanding the implications and repercussions of unfaithfulness in his own life situation. Hosea revealed to Israel that their problem was not about breaking the law. Their problem was that they were breaking the heart of God because they were breaking the sanctity of their covenant relationship.

*It is essential to remember that religious language, religious activity, and religious marketing are not substitutes for being still and knowing God in a personal relationship.*

In chapters four and following, we are introduced to the preaching of Hosea. He was a powerful preacher. His words are succinct and clear. His understanding of how to organize thoughts while anticipating the reflections of his listeners is noteworthy. In chapter four, Hosea used the setting of a court of law to introduce the complaints of God.

*Complaint #1:* You do not know me. God complains, *You express no faithfulness to me, you have no loyalty to me because I am not real to you* (4:1).

The people of God had become so absorbed in the many dimensions of life that they had lost an experiential relationship with the Lord. Like the demons, they believed in the existence of God. They had their religious life scheduled into their calendars. But they related to the Lord as a distant deity, a theological idea. They did not relate to the Lord as a living Being.

Is it possible that the church of today is drowning in religious information and thirsting for an experience of God? It is essential to remember that religious language, religious activity, and religious marketing are not substitutes for being still and knowing God in a personal relationship.

*Complaint #2:* Your crime rate is up. God complains, *You have no respect for my commandments and teachings, from the simplest virtues to the most heinous crime* (4:2).

The religious institution in Israelite culture was so interwoven into the fabric of their society that when religion went astray, the whole society did, too. The people of God were ignoring and abusing and violating every commandment. They were still teaching the commandments, still talking about them as though they were important, but they were not observing them. The result of their disobedience showed up in every area of cultural life. In everyday personal relationships and business dealings, they made false oaths and told lies to one another. In their community life, they committed murder and stole from one another. In their family life, adultery was rampant. The loss of character in the lives of the people kept spiraling downward until bloodshed became like a stream flowing through the land.

> *Church renewal will not occur by going inward, going upward, or going outward as long as the day-to-day obedience of the people of God continues to go downward.*

We must be careful to distinguish between the cultural context of Hosea's Israel and twenty-first century America. While some people propose that the life of America and the life of the church are the same thing, they are not. The wall of separation between church and state does not keep the two from influencing each other, but they are distinguishable. We would do better to compare Israel's situation with the state of the church, not the state and the church.

You do not have to look further than your local congregation or community to see that many people in the church give lip service to the way of the Lord, but not living service. Some people treat the church as though the church were an institution, rather than the breathing body of Christ in today's world. Therefore, they easily explain why they fail to keep the covenant of their calling, refuse to tell the truth, kill and steal the reputations of others, commit adultery, and in other ways contribute to the bloodstream of sin flowing through the church. Church renewal will not occur by going inward, going upward, or going outward as long as the day-to-day obedience of the people of God continues to go downward.

*Complaint #3:* You are killing my creation. God complains, *The earth has cried out to me saying that all living things are suffering; the animals, the birds, and even the fish are perishing* (4:3).

# Allowing the Bible to Point Beyond Itself

Jesus said to his religious opponents: "You search the scriptures because you think that in them you have eternal life; and it is they that testify on my behalf. Yet you refuse to come to me to have life" (John 5:39–40).

In essence, Jesus told them, *You are deeply focused on and committed to a study of Scripture because you think that you have a relationship with God through the words. These are the same Scriptures that point beyond themselves to me. Yet you refuse to come to me to have life in God.* As in the days of Hosea and Jesus, it is possible today to be religious, knowing the written words of God, and yet miss out on a personal relationship with the Living Word of God. This is it!

Baptists have, from their beginnings, heralded soul freedom of the individual. This Baptist principle is based on the premise that a personal relationship with God is the overarching concern when compared to diverse interpretations of words in Scripture.

---

Israel was connected to the land, but they forgot. Their sin had implications for all aspects of the Lord's creation. Their sin even had ecological effects. Their lack of responsibility and faithfulness was having an impact on the animals.

Today's church is behind the curve when it comes to making theological decisions and taking faithful actions related to the environment. Too often, congregations rebel against or violate laws and codes that have been established to protect the environment. The church should be taking care of ecosystems by living above the law rather than by looking for shortcuts and trying to live beyond the law.

> You do not have to look further than your local congregation or community to see that many people in the church give lip service to the way of the Lord, but not living service.

*Complaint #4:* You are playing religious games with my truth. God complains, *Those of you who are leaders of my people and those of you who follow the leaders of my people are both guilty of unfaithfulness and pretense* (4:4–12).

The priests of Israel were corrupt. The truth of God was not in them. They stumbled in broad daylight because they refused to be guided by God's light. Too, those who followed them were like the blind following the blind. The people of God confused faithfulness and worship with idolatry and superstition.

When leaders are corrupt or incompetent, the people have a problem. Leaders of today's church will be held accountable for their sincerity, humility, vulnerability, authenticity, honesty, and consistency in servanthood.

Yet, to look through much of the literature today and to hear many of today's church leaders, you might think they will be held accountable for their success, flamboyance, popularity, political savvy, and capacity to wield power. The religious business has never been more profitable for those who are in it for profit. The "people of God" who jump at any chance to get behind the next self-appointed superstar for Jesus, trendy big event using Jesus' name, or marketing blitz disguised as a God-breathed movement will find themselves with plenty to eat on their religious diet. Their appetite, however, will never be satisfied.

Between 4:13 and 7:16, Hosea continued to pronounce judgments on Israel and her leaders. In dialogue style, Israel offered a lament to the Lord (6:1–3). The Lord responded to their lack of sincerity by describing their expression of love to be like a morning cloud—present for a short time before it evaporates (6:4). God rejected their prayer of repentance because of its insincerity. The response of Israel was like a man who steps on your foot in a crowd and says, "I'm sorry," in a perfunctory manner as he keeps moving away from you. God said to Israel, through Hosea, "I desire steadfast love and not sacrifice, the knowledge of God rather than burnt offerings" (6:6). Hundreds of years later, Jesus would quote that verse as he gave the Pharisees a homework assignment, "Go and learn what this means, 'I desire mercy, not sacrifice'" (Matthew 9:13).

> *Today's church is behind the curve when it comes to making theological decisions and taking faithful actions related to the environment.*

The remainder of Hosea 6 through Hosea 7 tells the reasons Israel refused to heed God's warnings and continued to be guilty of God's charges against them. Their history of breaking the covenant made it difficult for them to see a new perspective (6:7—7:2). They tried to make themselves more secure by establishing political power networks (7:3–7). They diluted their trust in God by turning to other human alliances (7:8–12), and they were just plain rebellious (7:13–16).

## On Vulture's Wings (8:1–10, 14)

Hosea called on the trumpeter to sound the warning that rather than soaring on wings like eagles (Isaiah 40:31), Israel had vultures flying overhead. These vultures signified Israel's doom due to their breaking the covenant

# Thirteen Ways to Nurture Your Relationship with God

1. Be still and open to the voice of God.
2. Pray.
3. Worship.
4. Keep a journal.
5. Reflect or meditate on a passage of Scripture.
6. Pay close attention to nature (even if it is an inside plant).
7. Listen to a child describe a rainbow.
8. Sing (even if it is only a joyful noise).
9. Write poetry (even if it is terrible).
10. Write down a thanksgiving list.
11. Spend time with someone more than ninety years of age.
12. Let someone do something for you.
13. Do something for another person without letting the person know.

---

and transgressing the law (8:1). The people of God were saying to God, *We know you*, but their actions indicated the opposite (8:2–3). God charged that they had made decisions without consulting him. He rejected their manipulative ways (8:4). Too, God rejected their idols. In fact, the graven images made God angry (8:5–6).

The many ways that Israel had "spurned the good" (8:3) would result in catastrophe. The image of sowing the wind and reaping the whirlwind (8:7) points to the fact that the Lord was not bringing this catastrophe on Israel. Rather, Israel was bringing this catastrophe on themselves. The people of God did the sowing, and they would do the reaping. Too, while it might look as though there would be fruit to reap, "the standing grain has no heads, it shall yield no meal" (8:7). Israel was going to be "swallowed up," devoured, and would be seen

*The religious institution in Israelite culture was so interwoven into the fabric of their society that when religion went astray, the whole society did, too.*

to be a useless little people wandering around like a wild donkey all alone (8:8–9). "Israel has forgotten his Maker," using its resources to build palaces. The Southern Kingdom of Judah had built fortified cities to protect itself. But all of these efforts would fail (8:10, 14).

## Implications for Today

Nobody likes to get served an arrest warrant. In the prophetic preaching of Hosea, however, this is what occurred as God brought charges against the people of God. God's charges were strong. God's evidence against the Israelites was clear and well developed. Israel was guilty.

> The "people of God" who jump . . . to get behind the next self-appointed superstar for Jesus, trendy big event using Jesus' name, or marketing blitz disguised as a God-breathed movement . . . will never be satisfied.

Of course, that was then, and this is now. The question is not whether *Israel* was guilty, but whether *you* are guilty. Do you know God in a personal relationship? Are you focused on obeying the Lord's teachings and will for your life? Are you caring for all aspects of the Lord's teachings so as to impact all God's creation in a positive and life-nurturing way? Are you playing games with God's truth, chasing after trends and personalities, or are you expressing sincerity, humility, authenticity, vulnerability, honesty, and consistent servanthood?

If the finger of God is pointing at you and you are guilty as charged, I advise you to:

✱ A—Admit your guilt.
✱ B—Believe that God is merciful.
✱ C—Confess your sin honestly and fully.
✱ D—Dedicate yourself to a deeper discipleship.
✱ E—Entrust yourself to the will of God.
✱ F—Follow in the relationship with God that is revealed through Jesus Christ.

## QUESTIONS

1. What steps can you take, in your life and household, to assure that the Bible is not just read for spiritual information but is primarily used as a resource for spiritual formation? Can these steps be offered to your congregation in some way?

2. What do you do to nurture the vitality of your personal relationship with God?

3. Which of the following statements *best* represents your perspective?

   a. The church must focus on being transformed by the Spirit of God in order to be a change agent within the nation, like salt and light.

   b. The problems of our nation will never get better until we return this country to being a Christian nation by electing only Christians to office.

   c. Christians should seek to control and use every political, social, civil, judicial, and economic means possible to return this nation to God.

   d. The role of the church in America is to live humbly in relationship with God, live in obedience to the teachings and spiritual character of Christ, and continue the mission of God, as revealed through Christ.

4. When church leaders fail to be faithful, seek to manipulate the people of God, or lead through the power of their position rather than the power of their character, what actions should the church take toward them?

5. Which of God's complaints described in this lesson concern you most about the church today? Why? What can you, your class, or your congregation, do to make a difference?

## Focal Text

Hosea 11:1–11

## Background

Hosea 9:1–11:11

## Main Idea

In spite of their sins
against him, God does
not give up on people
but yearns to show
mercy to them.

*our* (handwritten)

*Thank you Father God* (handwritten)

## Question to Explore

When we have sinned,
does God want us back? *Yes* (handwritten)

## Study Aim

To identify implications of God's not giving up
on Israel in spite of their sins against him

## Study and Action Emphases

- Affirm the Bible as our authoritative guide
  for life and ministry
- Share the gospel with all people
- Develop a growing, vibrant faith
- Value all people as created in the image of
  God
- Encourage healthy families

# LESSON NINE

# God's Yearning Heart

## Quick Read

Through the good news according to Hosea, we
are reminded of the warm and tender compassion
that stirs within the heart of the Lord.

There should have been a phone call. When Bruce left, he said, "I will call when I get there." It was now 11 P.M., four hours after he should have arrived. Was he okay? Calling his cell phone was no help. There was just a recording saying the customer was not available. His apartment roommates had not seen him, but they promised they would give him the message.

Once again, Joe was up late thinking his son would call to stop his worrying. Once again, they had talked about these kinds of things over the weekend, and Bruce had said he understood. Once again, Bruce had promised that he was doing better, running around with a different crowd from the previous semester. Once again, he had assured his dad that his grades were better, his lifestyle was healthier, and his time management habits were more responsible. Once again, Joe knew that what his ears heard and what his heart felt gave him different signals.

Joe loved his son, but the frustration had occasionally overpowered his emotions. Ever since his wife, Wendy, died two years ago, he had yearned to have an even closer relationship with Bruce, their only child. In some ways, they were closer. Joe knew, though, that at least for now his role was being a giver without expecting anything in return. This was not like a few years ago, when Bruce wanted to be with his dad every day and stretched out his legs so as to step in his dad's footprints on the beach.

Joe just wanted Bruce to take life seriously. But Bruce refused to do so. Joe desired for Bruce to live his life as though he was aware that he had a future. Joe looked at the table in the foyer and down the hall. Everywhere he looked he saw Bruce's picture.

Suddenly Joe was startled by a sound. It was the clock striking midnight. There should have been a phone call.

## Hosea 11:1–11

1 When Israel was a child, I loved him,
and out of Egypt I called my son.
2 The more I called them,
the more they went from me;
they kept sacrificing to the Baals,
and offering incense to idols.
3 Yet it was I who taught Ephraim to walk,
I took them up in my arms;
but they did not know that I healed them.

<sup>4</sup> I led them with cords of human kindness,
with bands of love.
I was to them like those
who lift infants to their cheeks.
I bent down to them and fed them.
<sup>5</sup> They shall return to the land of Egypt,
and Assyria shall be their king,
because they have refused to return to me.
<sup>6</sup> The sword rages in their cities,
it consumes their oracle-priests,
and devours because of their schemes.
<sup>7</sup> My people are bent on turning away from me.
To the Most High they call,
but he does not raise them up at all.
<sup>8</sup> How can I give you up, Ephraim?
How can I hand you over, O Israel?
How can I make you like Admah?
How can I treat you like Zeboiim?
My heart recoils within me;
my compassion grows warm and tender.
<sup>9</sup> I will not execute my fierce anger;
I will not again destroy Ephraim;
for I am God and no mortal,
the Holy One in your midst,
and I will not come in wrath.
<sup>10</sup> They shall go after the LORD,
who roars like a lion;
when he roars,
his children shall come trembling from the west.
<sup>11</sup> They shall come trembling like birds from Egypt,
and like doves from the land of Assyria;
and I will return them to their homes, says the LORD.

## Be Sure Your Sin Will Find You Out (9:1—10:15)

Israel observed the religious festival of the harvest. But they were merely going through the motions of celebration. They did not experience the joy of thanksgiving; they merely experienced the addictions of unfaithfulness, including the emotions.

Hosea foretold of Israel's punishment that would come upon them despite their pretentious observances of religious traditions. Their punishment, according to Hosea, would include a failed harvest (9:2). Their worship of Baal, the fertility god, would prove futile. In addition, they would be destroyed or carried away into exile (9:3, 6). They would watch their children be slaughtered (9:11–14).

Their affluent and luxurious lifestyles would fade (10:1–2). Their political institutions would disappear (10:3). Their trust of one another would vanish, and litigation would increase (10:4).

Hosea called on Israel to seek the Lord by sowing righteousness in order that the rains of righteousness might fall on them and they could reap steadfast love (10:12). In 9:7, Hosea noted that Israel was aware of his message. Israel cried out that the prophet was a fool; they accused the man who spoke of spiritual things as being crazy. The response, recorded at the end of verse 7, records that Israel protested too much. Because Israel was fighting so hard against their guilt, they overreacted to the prophet. One of the worst intrusions into the rebellious life is the voice of truth that calls the rebel to responsibility for personal sin. Their sin had found them out.

> *The spiritual desires and cravings that reflect the mark of the image of God within each person will never be satisfied by pursuing the numbing goals of the senses.*

When rebellion is pursued, the results are never positive. There may be good feelings and fun times along the way. The desires and cravings of sinfulness may be satisfied. But, the rebel continues to live with an internal hollowness of despair. The spiritual desires and cravings that reflect the mark of the image of God within each person will never be satisfied by pursuing the numbing goals of the senses. Your sin will find you out.

## Parental Memories (11:1–4)

Through his preaching, Hosea pictured God in human ways and images. It is as though Hosea caught a glimmer of light in how to help Israel think relationally about God. The people of Israel had moved so far from a relationship with God as a living Being that they had no concept as to how they could begin anew. Hosea offered emotional, relational images of God.

> *There should have been a phone call.*

First, Hosea used his marriage to the prostitute, Gomer, in an effort to help Israel see how they were hurting God by their unfaithfulness. Now, in chapter 11, Hosea offered the image of a loving Father seeking to express love to a wayward son. For the Christian reader, there are times when it seems as though these words could be titled, "The Gospel of Hosea."

We have a difficult time understanding how unusual this image of God as Father would have been for Israel. We look backward at this prophecy through the lens of Jesus' teachings. We know that Jesus taught us to pray, "Our Father" (Matthew 6:9). We know the parable of the prodigal (Luke 15:11–32). We know Jesus cried out from the cross, "Father, forgive them," and "Father, into your hands I commend my spirit" (Luke 23:34, 46). Even so, for a prophet trying to get the attention of the people of God, this way of thinking about God was thought-provoking.

*When a parent expresses love to a child and yet the child desires no relationship with the parent, the parent is left with nothing but pain and memories.*

Hosea pictured the Lord involved in a reflective moment. Perhaps you can imagine the Lord sitting on the back porch remembering Israel as a child. Parental memories were running through the mind of God. The Lord remembered the loving relationship with Israel when, hundreds of years earlier, Israel was called out of Egypt to take a walk with Dad toward home (11:1).

However, not all parental memories are pleasant, are they? The more God called to Israel, the farther they moved away from the Lord. The interdependent covenant to which Israel was called had not been packed in the suitcase for the trip. Instead, Israel packed independence and never

## Ephraim

Ephraim was the name given to one of the regions of Israel. Ephraim was the younger son born to Joseph and Joseph's Egyptian wife, Asenath (Genesis 41:52). Ephraim, along with his older brother Manasseh, received a tribal inheritance along with the sons of Jacob (Gen. 48:1–5).

The region of Israel named for Ephraim was bordered to the west by the Mediterranean Sea, to the north by the tribe of Manasseh, to the east by the Jordan River and to the south by the tribe of Benjamin. After the fall of Israel to Assyria in 733 BC, only Ephraim and western Manasseh were left to the king of Israel (see 2 Kings 15:29). In time, due to the important cities and sites in the land of Ephraim, many began to refer to Israel as Ephraim. In Hosea, there are many passages where the modern reader is surprised to find the name Ephraim rather than the name Israel.

*[handwritten margin notes: "ourselves as children of God", "I am God", "Sorry Father", "God"]*

expressed any intent except to do their own thing, please themselves, take the easy road, and complain when they got into trouble. Israel was especially difficult when they were asked to make a sacrifice or be responsible for their actions.

For the most part, Israel welcomed the opportunity to be free from bondage. But Israel attached themselves to an empty relationship with Baal, a non-being from which nothing had been received and from which nothing could be expected. Israel was an especially loved child of the Lord who refused to be childlike and yet was ever childish (11:2).

> The nature of God is not anger, destruction, or wrath. The nature of God is love.

*[handwritten margin notes: "Dan.", "ourselves"]*

What weighs heavily on the heart of a loving parent is a child who does not return the parent's love. When a parent expresses love to a child and yet the child desires no relationship with the parent, the parent is left with nothing but pain and memories.

The Lord enumerated memories of Israel's childhood. The Father held the hand of the child as the child started to take his first steps. When the child would fall, the Father would pick the child up in his arms. The Father would bring healing to the hurts of the child, but the child was so self-centered that he was oblivious to the help. The Father provided gentle direction and leadership in the life of the child through lovingkindness and mercy. The Father related to the maturing child as though he were an infant being lifted to the cheek of the parent for reassurance and comfort. The Father would always lower himself to provide for the health and growth of the child (11:3–4).

## Parental Frustration (11:5–7)

Many parents of teenagers and young adults have moved, in a flash, from warm reflections on their child's early years to utter frustration over their child's expressions of arrogance and pride. The tone from verse 4 to verse 5 represents such a sudden shift.

*[handwritten margin notes: "Dan.", "ourselves"]*

Verses 5–7 report the Lord's frustration over Israel's lack of faithful response to divine initiative. The future suffering that Israel would experience was not due to parental punishment by the Father but to childish decisions by Israel, the son. Because Israel refused to return to the Lord, they would be overcome by Assyria. Repeatedly, Israel declined to live humbly in their relationship toward the Lord.

Punishment would come through conquest by foreign nations. Policies during the reign of Hoshea ben Elah of Israel were pro-Egyptian (see 2 Kings 17:1–6; reigned 732–721 BC). He hoped that an alliance with the Egyptian Pharaoh would free Israel from Assyrian rule. This policy would eventually result in destruction and suffering by either Egypt or Assyria. In 733, Tiglath-pileser III of Assyria took over most of Israel's territory. Assyria ruled Israel, and the Assyrian swords brought much destruction to Israel during these military campaigns. Because of Israel's scheming alliance with Egypt, Assyria made Israel suffer.

The Lord lamented the fact that Israel continued to turn away from a faithful relationship with the living God. Even through the suffering, Israel refused to turn to the Lord. Israel continued to call on Baal, but this non-existent deity could not do anything for them. This continual refusal to acknowledge the Lord made the Father of Israel weary. The reader can sense that the Lord was ready to just give the son up to his own self-destructive behaviors. The sense in the story is that the Lord is ready to let the son go his own way (11:7). Enough is enough!

> *God hates sin but never the sinner.*

## The Heart of God (11:8–9)

Despite the constant rebellion of Israel, the Lord refused to give up. The Lord's heart just could not give up on Israel. These two verses (11:8–9) reveal the core character of God as much as any two verses in prophetic literature.

One after another, the prophets warned and called the people of God to give attention to faithfulness and righteousness. Yet the hardened hearts of God's people refused to heed the warnings or humble themselves before the Lord.

What parent of a rebellious child has not entered a silent, inner conversation? At just the moment that a loving parent decides that this repeated pain and suffering must end, the love becomes stronger. The parent's heart keeps hoping and keeps believing. Just when the parent's frustration reaches the point of no return, the loving heart enables the parent to stop short of doing irreparable damage to the potential relationship with the child.

A parent would be likely to give up on a child like Israel, who showed as little respect for the parent and as little remorse over his childish sin and

# Case Study

In the introduction, you met Joe, a father with a yearning heart for his son Bruce. Joe has prayed for Bruce, sent Bruce notes of encouragement, hidden notes in his laundry and book bag, and told him, "I love you," with hugs over and over again. Joe's heart is hurting, and he needs to talk to a friend. He approaches you with tears in his eyes. What can you offer?

unfaithfulness.)While the depth of human parental love cannot be measured, there is a limit to how far a parent can go before breaking. Initially, the voice of the Lord is expressed in the form of divided feelings. This division of emotions portrays a person who is immobilized from action. This Father, tired yet hopeful, stressed yet faithful, is perplexed and ready to give up on the child.

*God loves you no matter how tragic you have made your life, no matter how extreme your rebellion, and no matter how complete your sin.*

However, Hosea clarified that God is not mortal. Even when the Lord desired to give up on the people of God, the core of God's character is love and would not allow God to be untrue to God's self. Deuteronomy 21:18–21 provides the teaching of the law to guide parents who had an abusive son. According to the law, a rebellious son was to be brought to the elders of the city to be stoned to death. Be thankful that Jesus revealed to us the Father as pictured in Hosea, rather than as described in the law of Deuteronomy.

Notice that verse 9 contains a threefold declaration of God's intent:

- "I will not execute my fierce anger"
- "I will not again destroy"
- "I will not come in wrath"

The nature of God is not anger, destruction, or wrath. The nature of God is love.

## The Homecoming (11:10–11)

In literature, music, drama, and movies, the homecoming stirs emotions of joy as people are described or shown with broad smiles, running toward one another and embracing. For the rebel, home is a place from which to escape, imprisoning his or her freedom and individualistic desires. For the rebel on the return home, the perspective is different. For the rebel who is involved in a homecoming, home is a place where relationships are tended, a place to move beyond the mistakes of the past, a place to be prepared for the long journey ahead.

After Israel passed through the time of punishment, they would hear the voice of the Lord. Notice the difference in language. When running away from the Lord, it is at Israel's initiative. When returning home, it is because the Lord says, "I will return them to their homes" (11:11).

## Implications for Today

God hates sin but never the sinner. As a loving parent, the heart of God grieves, gets angry, expresses frustration, punishes disobedience, and allows suffering to soften the heart of a child. But God never abandons a child. Even the most rebellious child in the family will never be abandoned.

Warm and tender compassion stirs within the heart of God. God loves you no matter how tragic you have made your life, no matter how extreme your rebellion, and no matter how complete your sin. You cannot become bad enough to change the character of God. You cannot sin enough to cause God to stop loving you. If you are being unfaithful and pretentious in your relationship with God, hoping that God will leave you alone and stop loving you, you are wasting your time.

*If you are being unfaithful and pretentious in your relationship with God, hoping that God will leave you alone and stop loving you, you are wasting your time.*

You might as well give it up and respond to the love of God. God welcomes you home—not merely to an address or a place but to a relationship.

## QUESTIONS

1. What have you learned about the Lord through rebellion? What have you learned about the Lord by having to deal with rebellion in others?

2. When you know you have been unfaithful to the Lord, how do you know? How do you deal with conviction and guilt?

3. In what ways would your relationship with God be different if Jesus Christ had not revealed the nature of God to the world?

4. How has the church relied on human or political alliances in attempts to secure itself, rather than relying on the Lord?

5. How should God's yearning heart be evident in and expressed by God's missional church today in relating with rebellious people?

## Focal Text

Hosea 14

## Background

Hosea 11:12—14:9

## Main Idea

God offers restoration and abundant new life to people who return to him.

## Question to Explore

What hope is there when the sentence is "guilty as charged"?

## Study Aim

To decide how I will respond to God's invitation to return to him

## Study and Action Emphases

- Affirm the Bible as our authoritative guide for life and ministry
- Share the gospel with all people
- Develop a growing, vibrant faith

## LESSON TEN

# Return to the Lord

## Quick Read

Merely setting goals or changing behavior does not provide spiritual renewal. Spiritual renewal involves your spiritual work of repentance and the renewal work of the Lord.

Traveling with their husbands to a company conference, Joyce and Bonnie were prepared to enjoy the scenery of eastern Tennessee and western North Carolina. The rain, though, would not stop. Fog obscured the mountains. In the lobby of the hotel, they picked up several brochures and fliers describing local places of interest, restaurants to enjoy, and shops to explore. They decided to take the day to browse antique stores. Since they were from Minnesota, they expected to find several unique items in these Southern shops.

At dinner, the wives told their husbands about their day. In the conversation, Bonnie asked Joyce, "Did you notice what almost every store operator said to us as we left?" Joyce replied, "Yes, I noticed what they said, but what impressed me most was the sincerity in their voices. It was like they really meant it." *In the heart & faith*

Each shop owner had enjoyed their Scandinavian accents, but these women enjoyed listening to the slow talk of these kind Southerners. Their husbands took the bait and asked, "What did they say?"

Bonnie looked at Joyce, the women leaned their faces together, and in their best Scandinavian "Southernese" said, "Y'all come back now."

*How far father have I strayed?* Through Hosea, the Lord reminded the people of Israel how far they had strayed from a relationship with the Lord. Through Hosea, the Lord called out to Israel. Desiring Israel to be a recipient of grace, the Lord said something like, *Y'all come back now,* by calling the nation to repentance.

*open my ears that I might hear you calling.*

# Hosea 14

1 Return, O Israel, to the LORD your God,
  for you have stumbled because of your iniquity.
2 Take words with you
  and return to the LORD;
  say to him,
  "Take away all guilt;
  accept that which is good,
  and we will offer
  the fruit of our lips.
3 Assyria shall not save us;
  we will not ride upon horses;
  we will say no more, 'Our God,'
  to the work of our hands.
  In you the orphan finds mercy."

4 I will heal their disloyalty;
   I will love them freely,
   for my anger has turned from them.
5 I will be like the dew to Israel;
   he shall blossom like the lily,
   he shall strike root like the forests of Lebanon.
6 His shoots shall spread out;
   his beauty shall be like the olive tree,
   and his fragrance like that of Lebanon.
7 They shall again live beneath my shadow,
   they shall flourish as a garden;
   they shall blossom like the vine,
   their fragrance shall be like the wine of Lebanon.
8 O Ephraim, what have I to do with idols?
   It is I who answer and look after you.
   I am like an evergreen cypress;
   your faithfulness comes from me.
9 Those who are wise understand these things;
   those who are discerning know them.
   For the ways of the LORD are right,
   and the upright walk in them,
   but transgressors stumble in them.

*[Handwritten margin note: plant me deep into the root of the vine which is (Jesus) so that I might grow and produce good and pleasing fruit for you Father God.]*

*[Handwritten note: give me]*

*[Handwritten note: make me]*

*[Handwritten note: May I walk upright and not stumble.]*

## Warning Signs on the Road Away from God (11:12—13:16)

Israel did not arrive at the place of estrangement from the Lord without warnings or directions. Israel ignored every road sign on their journey away from a sincere relationship with God. Through our study of Hosea, we have read several of the signs ignored by Israel. Perhaps we have been perplexed as to how Israel could miss the warnings and corrections. Do we, however, do any better at reading the signs in our lives and in our times? *[Handwritten: No!]* Are there similarities between the signs of Hosea's time and today? *[Handwritten: yes!]*

Almost like a driver's manual, the thirty-one verses from Hosea 11:12—13:16 picture the signs Israel ignored. Israel should have recognized these signs to be warnings, if not evidence, that they were going the wrong way, traveling away from God. There was lying, falsehood, violence, false security, oppression, pride, selfishness, pretense, misrepresentation, manipulation, moral relativism, deception, materialism, laziness, idolatry, and a general attitude of dissatisfaction.

*[Handwritten margin note: turn me around Father God that I might go in the right direction that leads to you!]*

# The Invitation

Each Sunday, most Baptist congregations extend an invitation at the end of worship. The pastor or preacher of the day invites people to make public their decisions and commitments to follow Jesus Christ as Savior and Lord. During this time of worship the movement of the Spirit of the Lord may become visible as people move toward the front of the sanctuary to pray and/or inform another believer of their repentance, commitment, or intention.

This tradition of extending an invitation makes a pivotal statement about the Baptist principle of accountability for one's personal relationship with the Lord. Some refer to this principle as soul freedom or soul competency. The weekly invitation is a reminder to each worshiper that one's walk with the Lord is an individual responsibility. The invitation should never be used to manipulate a person. Neither should the invitation be minimized as an interlude between sermon and lunch. It should be valued as a reminder of the need of repentance throughout one's life, as inspired by the Spirit of God.

Through experiences, prophets, visions, and parables, the Lord had sought Israel's attention, to no avail. Israel thought the way to get rid of guilt was to stay so busy in life that they could keep guilt at a distance. By continuing to live at a numbing pace, pursuing wealth, manipulating the truth, enjoying recreation more than work, fostering false security with human political alliances, paying attention to every religious tradition by turning spiritual festivals into social happenings, Israel was able to downplay the general attitude of dissatisfaction that covered the land like a pall.

> *Think about it.*
>
> To become involved in religious activities without being humble is to be shallow and dishonest.

## Turn Around (14:1)

As Hosea's collection of sermons comes to the last chapter, the prophet called on Israel to do a U-turn. Hosea challenged Israel to repent. Israel was challenged to turn around from pursuing iniquity to travel in the opposite direction, toward the Lord.

When you look back at the unfaithfulness of Israel, you wonder why the people did not see their misery and change their ways. Several years ago, I was introduced to a proverb attributed to Albert Einstein. It goes something like this: *Insanity is doing the same thing the same way over and over and over again and expecting a different result.* For Israel, their lack of initiative toward the Lord was insanity. But before we are too critical, we must admit that we are often like these people, living as though we do not know how to repent.

*Without much serious thought, you can begin to think that religious activity and congregational involvement are the pinnacles of religious commitment.*

On one occasion, a soldier was asked, "Can you explain what happened when you came to Christ?" According to the story, the soldier replied, "It was as though I heard a Voice inside of me say four things: 'Attention!' 'Halt!' 'About-face!' 'Forward march!'" In order to return to the Lord, one must give full attention to the voice of the Lord, stop walking in the way of unfaithfulness and iniquity, turn around to face the opposite direction (repent), and begin to walk in the footsteps of the Lord as revealed in Jesus Christ.

*[handwritten: It is a true real relationship with Jesus.]*

## The Words of Repentance (14:2–3)

Israel was accustomed to approaching Baal with rams and lambs to offer sacrifices in seeking the favor of the idol. Hosea called Israel to return to the Lord, not with animals, but with words. The words needed to be honest words of confession reflecting true repentance.

To turn around and return to the Lord is part of true repentance. But, upon arriving in the Presence of the Lord, there is a need to express contrition of the spirit. To become involved in religious activities without being humble is to be shallow and dishonest. God can see the spirit of the individual and know the true motives and desires.

This teaching should remind us to be on guard against one of the biggest temptations in modern Christianity. It's this: *Being active or even semi-active in a congregation can get in the way of an authentic relationship with God.* Without much serious thought, you can begin to think that religious activity and congregational involvement are the pinnacles of religious commitment. Hosea reminded the people of God of his day and today that this is far from the truth.

You do not have to be an evil person to be in need of approaching God with words of repentance. You need not be a criminal, a juvenile delinquent, or a problem employee to realize your need to offer to God words of repentance. You may even be on the church finance committee. You may take covered dishes to people when their relatives die. You may volunteer to teach Vacation Bible School or be a counselor at church camp. You may be a section leader in the choir. You may feed the homeless in a soup kitchen. You may be active in the prayer ministry of your church. But your level of religious activity is unimpressive to God. An honest, authentic relationship with God is nurtured by turning to God in repentance.

Repentance is the word we use to describe the evidence of spiritual transformation. If people tell us they are sorry, we tend to be unsure of their sincerity, especially if the hurt is deep. We find out over time whether their words represented an apology or true repentance. An apology tells us they are sorry. Repentance tells us they are sorry and they will make every effort to avoid hurting us again in the future.

*. . . Many Christians have become more focused on the programs of church life than on their relationship with God.*

Amen!

After you fail to obey the lordship of Christ in some area of your life, you may feel guilty. This feeling is the Spirit of God convicting your spirit of your sin as you fall short of God's ideal for your life. As you confess your sin to God, you acknowledge your accountability for your failure, and you express to God that you do not want to repeat your sin.

The problem is that many Christians have become more focused on the programs of church life than on their relationship with God. They do not intend for life to become this way. In fact, for most of them, they have no idea that they live this way. This way of life is all they have known for so long that it seems normal. But be warned, this was the case in the days of Hosea. How long has it been since you offered authentic words of repentance to the Lord? How long has it been since you took an honest spiritual inventory of the closeness of your relationship with God?

## How the Lord Responds to Repentance (14:4–5a)

These verses reveal three important images of God's character. Each image carried meaning for the people of Hosea's day and enlightens today's church about the character and will of God.

First, there is the image of God as healer (14:4). Unfaithfulness does not just disappear because a person says, *I am going to be faithful now*. Because unfaithfulness is a spiritual matter, the Lord is the only one who can heal unfaithfulness. Spiritual healing is God's work. Only God can bring about spiritual wholeness and health. Some healings are instantaneous; most occur over a lengthy period of time. After repentance, God is committed to bring about healing in a person's life no matter how long it takes.

Second, there is the image of God as lover (14:4). The Lord is unlike the lifeless idols of Baal worship. With the Lord, there are no requirements to earn the Lord's favor. In a relationship with the Lord, once there is repentance, love can be received freely. Through Hosea, the character of God is described in similar fashion to the way in which God is revealed in Christ and the writings of the New Testament—"God is love" (1 John 4:16).

Third, there is the image of God as life-giver (14:5a). People in the time of Hosea knew nothing of running water through pipes to a faucet. They could nourish their vegetation with water from a well, experience sporadic rains, or dig irrigation channels. The dew, though, was a constant. Then as now, dew simply appeared each morning to nourish and refresh. After you repent and are on the other side of the darkness of sin, the Lord greets you each morning—nourishing, refreshing, and giving you life.

We often talk in churches these days about mission statements, re-visioning processes, strategic planning, and goal setting. These have their place. It is essential to remember that spiritual transformation and spiritual renewal are quite different, however. Spiritual life does not change just because we set goals or rearrange the behaviors and priorities of our lives. The only way for us to experience spiritual transformation or spiritual renewal is to become attentive to the Lord, repent of our unfaithfulness, and claim the work of God on our behalf. God will then heal us of our spiritual pain, express gracious love to us, and bring nourishing refreshment into our lives.

> *Only God can bring about spiritual wholeness and health.*

## The Results of Repentance (14:5b–7)

The Israelites participated in a fertility cult. Hosea turned their familiarity with these images into a description of how life changes after the Lord responds to sincere repentance.

After you repent and the Lord responds to your sincerity, your life is transformed. Your life will begin to blossom and flourish. Like the lily,

# Think About It

Last Friday evening, as you were beginning your weekend, how much time did you give to considering what would be the Scriptures, hymns, and prayers used to guide worship later that evening at the Jewish synagogue? Most likely, you gave about the same amount of reflection time to worship in the synagogue last Friday evening that most people in your community gave to worship in your church's sanctuary last Sunday morning. What does your church do to connect people with God's invitation to return to a relationship with the Lord?

whose root can shoot forth numerous bulbs, you will find your life becoming a work of beauty. After the Lord responds to your repentance, you will be well anchored, with deep roots like the forests of Lebanon. Your life will be like the cedars of Lebanon, having deep roots to provide strength and stability.

Following the Lord's response to your repentance, your life will become useful, and your influence will be widespread. Your usefulness and your influence will mature as you depend on the Lord for continual honesty and authenticity in your relationship with God, The prayer of Jesus is our model for Christian discipleship, "Not my will, but yours be done" (Luke 22:42).

> The only way for us to experience spiritual transformation or spiritual renewal is to become attentive to the Lord, repent of our unfaithfulness, and claim the work of God on our behalf.

The imagery of nature continues as Hosea referred to the beauty of the olive tree and the sweet fragrance of the cedar forests in Lebanon. When the Lord responds to your repentance, your life will become known for the beauty of its character and the sweetness of its effect. Your life will flourish like a garden in the shade, protected from extreme heat.

## The Sermon's Invitation (14:8–9)

In these last two verses, Hosea revealed the Lord to have a loving face and outstretched arms toward the unfaithful people. The Lord had condemned their sin, revealed divine love, and invited the people to return to the relationship of faithfulness. Hosea finished the collection of sermons with one last plea.

Let me paraphrase what I believe the Lord was saying, as follows:

*I do not relate with you through the superstitions of idols and religious busyness. In a direct Spirit-with-spirit relationship, I speak with you, and I look after you. I am faithful to you. Even your capacity to have faith is a gift from me. If you are wise, you understand what I am saying. In your spirit, you are able to discern what I mean. You know that my ways are the right way to live, and you know how to live by them. You also know that to live by any other way will cause your life to stumble.*

Christians can see Jesus leaning forward to people weary from meaningless and empty religious activity and saying, "Come to me, all you that are weary and carrying heavy burdens, and I will give you rest" (Matthew 11:28).

## Implications for Today

A few months ago, I was visiting a ninety-eight-year-old man. His mind was alert, and his health was good. We talked about all the many changes he had witnessed over the past century. Then I asked, "Out of everything you have seen, what surprises you most?" His response surprised me. He said, "I guess what has surprised me most is how many people seem to do everything they can do to make their lives as difficult and miserable as possible."

> *"I guess what has surprised me most is how many people seem to do everything they can do to make their lives as difficult and miserable as possible."*

By continuing to live at a numbing pace, pursuing wealth, manipulating the truth, enjoying leisure and recreation more than work, fostering false security with human political alliances, changing every religious tradition from worship into a social happening, Israel tried to downplay the general attitude of religious dissatisfaction that covered the land like a pall. How could they have missed all the signs?

How can we, though, miss all the signs? We have heard the Lord say, *Y'all come back now,* haven't we?

# QUESTIONS

1. Do you see any of the signs of Hosea's time among the people of God today? If so, how are we responding to the signs?

2. How do you define *repentance?*

3. What makes repentance difficult for the Christian? Is this different for a non-Christian?

4. In what ways does our technological society move us away from or toward a deeper relationship with the Lord? What role does repentance have in this deeper relationship?

5. In your experience, how is one's life different after repentance to the Lord?

6. Even if someone has seemed to do everything possible to make his or her life difficult and miserable, how can repentance help bring healing, grace, and new life?

# Introducing

## MICAH: *What the Lord Requires*

"What does the Lord require of you?" So asks one of the most famous passages in all of the Bible. The question is found in Micah 6:8. In no uncertain terms, Micah stated what the Lord required. Moreover, Micah indicated that the people who called themselves God's people had not met the Lord's requirements.

As the prophets Amos and Hosea had also charged, Micah declared that God's people had knowingly failed to be faithful to God. Micah accused them of having coveted property that was not theirs and of having engaged in underhanded means to take it for themselves. Furthermore, even the religious leaders—priests and prophets—as well as the governmental leaders—rulers and judges—had sold out to the system. Judgment day was coming.

Even in the midst of the people's evils and God's coming punishment, however, Micah extended a word of hope, one of the most memorable in all of the Bible. God would eventually bring peace. The nation, indeed all the nations, would "beat their swords into plowshares" (4:3).[1] Too, God would provide a ruler unlike the faithless, greedy rulers Micah condemned. This ruler, understood by Christians to be Jesus the Christ, would be "the one of peace" (5:5).

Micah's prophecies likely came beginning in the 720s prior to the destruction of the Northern Kingdom in 722 BC and extending to around the time of the invasion of Judah in 701 BC by Sennacherib, the Assyrian ruler. Amos and Hosea, slightly earlier than Micah, had directed their messages mainly toward the Northern Kingdom. Micah 1:1 states that Micah's messages are directed toward (1:1) both "Samaria" (referring to the Northern Kingdom) and "Jerusalem" (referring to the Southern Kingdom, Judah). The Book of Micah thus speaks to "Israel," the whole people of God, both the Northern Kingdom and the Southern Kingdom.

Perhaps the greatest emphasis is on Judah, the Southern Kingdom. Micah's messages continued to speak with power to the surviving portion of Israel, the Southern Kingdom, on into the time when Judah faced God's judgment at the hand of Babylon in the sixth century BC.

In lesson eleven, the first lesson on the Book of Micah, Micah condemns the greedy acts of covetousness that were wreaking such havoc on people (1:1–7; 2:1–9). Lesson twelve, from Micah 3, focuses on the greediness of even the political and religious leaders. Lesson thirteen, the third lesson from Micah, considers the peace God promised and yet promises to people who will be faithful to him (4:1–8; 5:2–5a). Lesson fourteen, on Micah 6:1–8, features God's lawsuit against his people and asks and answers one of the greatest questions of life (6:8), "What does the Lord require?"

## MICAH: WHAT THE LORD REQUIRES

| | | |
|---|---|---|
| Lesson 11 | Where Coveting Leads | Micah 1:1–7; 2:1–9 |
| Lesson 12 | When Leaders Sell Out | Micah 3 |
| Lesson 13 | Peace Is Coming | Micah 4:1–8; 5:2–5a |
| Lesson 14 | God's Case Against His People | Micah 6:1–8 |

Additional Resources for Studying the Book of Micah:[2]

James Limburg. "Micah." *Interpretation: A Bible Commentary for Teaching and Preaching*. Atlanta: John Knox Press, 1988.

B. Elmo Scoggin. "Micah." *The Broadman Bible Commentary*. Volume 7. Nashville, Tennessee: Broadman Press, 1972.

Daniel J. Simundson. "Micah." *The New Interpreter's Bible*. Volume VII. Nashville: Abingdon Press, 1996.

Ralph L. Smith. "Micah." *Word Biblical Commentary*. Volume 32. Waco, Texas: Word Books, Publisher, 1984.

Hans Walter Wolff. *Micah: A Commentary*. Translated by Gary Stansell. Minneapolis: Augsburg, 1990.

Hans Walter Wolff. *Micah the Prophet*. Translated by Ralph D. Gehrke. Philadelphia: Fortress Press, 1981.

## NOTES

1.  Unless otherwise indicated, all Scripture quotations in "Introducing Micah" and the lessons on Micah are from the New Revised Standard Version Bible, copyright 1989, Division of Christian Education of the National Council of the Churches of Christ in the United States of America. Used by permission. All rights reserved.
2.  Listing a book does not imply full agreement by the writers or BAPTISTWAY PRESS® with all of its comments.

## Focal Text

Micah 1:1–7; 2:1–9

## Background

Micah 1—2

## Main Idea

God judges people who oppress others in their desire to have more things for themselves.

## Question to Explore

What place does the desire for things really have in your life?

## Study Aim

To relate God's condemnation of coveting to my life situation

## Study and Action Emphases

- Affirm the Bible as our authoritative guide for life and ministry
- Develop a growing, vibrant faith
- Value all people as created in the image of God
- Encourage healthy families
- Obey and serve Jesus by meeting physical, spiritual, and emotional needs

# LESSON ELEVEN

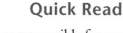

# Where Coveting Leads

## Quick Read

God holds us responsible for our desires as well as our actions. Desires to have what is not ours as well as the actions that flow from these desires are under the judgment of God and have within themselves the seeds of destruction.

Coveting can occur in unexpected places. The manager of a Christian bookstore run by Baptists in a city in Peru worked every day with Baptist missionaries from the United States. He admired the cars they drove in their mission work. He likely did not realize that the missionaries did not own these things but that they were the property of the Baptist Mission. Nevertheless, he wanted to have such things, too. Eventually he did. He acquired a large home and began driving a new car. It was then discovered that he had embezzled thousands upon thousands of dollars over the years. That city almost lost its Christian bookstore, and the reputation of Baptists was damaged.

We are saddened when we hear of someone in a trusted position who takes advantage of that trust to misappropriate funds. We know the reality of one person or group who want the power they perceive in another's position. They may use rumor, half-truths, and lies to take their place. Whether such power struggles occur in a local church or at the national level, here in the United States or on the mission field, they result from covetousness, and they damage the Christian witness of God's people.

Covetousness is greed made personal. If greed is expressed in the words, "I want things," then covetousness is expressed in the words, "I want *your* things."

Micah, an eighth-century prophet, confronted and condemned coveting (Micah 2:2). He was certainly not the first to see the destructive power of covetousness at work when one of God's people oppresses another in an effort to seize what is desired. From the time of Moses, the people of Israel knew God's word, "Thou shalt not covet . . ." (Exodus 20:17, KJV). The Northern Kingdom of Israel had witnessed the abuse of power that leads even to murder when King Ahab coveted Naboth's vineyard (1 Kings 21). Micah's voice, however, still speaks clearly to our generation in which the desire for things is as strong as ever.

# Micah 1:1–7

¹The word of the LORD that came to Micah of Moresheth in the days of Kings Jotham, Ahaz, and Hezekiah of Judah, which he saw concerning Samaria and Jerusalem.
² Hear, you peoples, all of you;
   listen, O earth, and all that is in it;
   and let the Lord GOD be a witness against you,
   the Lord from his holy temple.

3 For lo, the LORD is coming out of his place,
and will come down and tread upon the high places of the earth.
4 Then the mountains will melt under him
and the valleys will burst open,
like wax near the fire,
like waters poured down a steep place.
5 All this is for the transgression of Jacob
and for the sins of the house of Israel.
What is the transgression of Jacob?
Is it not Samaria?
And what is the high place of Judah?
Is it not Jerusalem?
6 Therefore I will make Samaria a heap in the open country,
a place for planting vineyards.
I will pour down her stones into the valley,
and uncover her foundations.
7 All her images shall be beaten to pieces,
all her wages shall be burned with fire,
and all her idols I will lay waste;
for as the wages of a prostitute she gathered them,
and as the wages of a prostitute they shall again be used.

# Micah 2:1–9

1 Alas for those who devise wickedness
and evil deeds on their beds!
When the morning dawns, they perform it,
because it is in their power.
2 They covet fields, and seize them;
houses, and take them away;
they oppress householder and house,
people and their inheritance.
3 Therefore thus says the LORD:
Now, I am devising against this family an evil
from which you cannot remove your necks;
and you shall not walk haughtily,
for it will be an evil time.
4 On that day they shall take up a taunt song against you,
and wail with bitter lamentation,
and say, "We are utterly ruined;
the LORD alters the inheritance of my people;

how he removes it from me!
Among our captors he parcels out our fields."
5 Therefore you will have no one to cast the line by lot
in the assembly of the LORD.
6 "Do not preach"—thus they preach—
"one should not preach of such things;
disgrace will not overtake us."
7 Should this be said, O house of Jacob?
Is the LORD's patience exhausted?
Are these his doings?
Do not my words do good
to one who walks uprightly?
8 But you rise up against my people as an enemy;
you strip the robe from the peaceful,
from those who pass by trustingly
with no thought of war.
9 The women of my people you drive out
from their pleasant houses;
from their young children you take away
my glory forever.

## God's Word Through God's Prophet (1:1)

The Book of Micah is a part of what the Hebrew Bible knows as the Book of the Twelve (which includes books sometimes referred to as the minor prophets). The introduction to the Book of Micah (1:1) thus shares many features with the introductions of other prophetic books. These introductions may have been shaped by the editor of the whole collection to give the reader of the whole a context with which to understand each part.

This first verse of the Book of Micah dates the prophet in the latter half of the eighth century BC. Micah takes his place among the other great writing prophets of that time—Amos, Hosea, and Isaiah—as he interprets the events around 722 BC that focused on the fall of Samaria and the end of the Northern Kingdom of Israel. Micah means *Who is like the Lord?* Other than the prophet's name and his hometown (probably Moresheth-Gath, 1:14), we are told nothing about the prophet himself. What is told is that he is a spokesman for the Lord God of Israel. God's word, not the person who speaks it, is the focus of the text. His message has a dual context. It is "concerning Samaria and Jerusalem."

This introduction by an editor from the time of the Babylonian exile alerts us to the three stages of the message of Micah. There is a time of Micah's ministry before 722 in which he preached to the Northern Kingdom, urging them to recognize their sin and repent. The second stage is the time of Micah's preaching to Judah between 722 and 701 (the year of Sennacherib's siege of Jerusalem, see 2 Kings 18:9—19:37; Isaiah 36—37). In this stage Micah interpreted the fate of Samaria in order to warn Jerusalem that the Southern Kingdom, too, must acknowledge its sin and

*Coveting can occur in unexpected places.*

turn back to the Lord. The third stage came more than 150 years later, after the fall of Jerusalem at the hands of the Babylonian Empire, and continues to this day as Micah's message comes even to us. The catastrophes God's people experienced in the fall of both Samaria and Jerusalem indicate God's willingness to judge even his own. Thus all the peoples and nations of the earth should be warned so that they might turn to the Lord in repentance.

## Here Comes the Judge (1:2–5)

Verse 2 sounds like the initiation of the Hebrew judicial process with a call for the village elders to gather and hear a lawsuit. Micah of Moresheth would have participated in this type of trial. The plaintiff would stand at the city gate and call to the men as they were going out to their fields to work. They, as well as other residents, would stop to listen to the charges and consider the evidence.

This trial, however, was no local matter. The summons was given to all the peoples of the earth, and the aggrieved party calling the court into session was the Lord (1:2)! More surprisingly, the defendants named were Samaria and Jerusalem, the centers of power of God's own people (1:5). The lawsuit that God brought against his own people had global significance.

The second half of verse two can be translated, *The Lord God will be among you as a witness, the Lord from his holy temple.* The term "witness" comes from the Hebrew verb that means *to testify, to inform,* or *to warn.* God called forth all the peoples of the earth in order to warn them of their impending judgment through the example of God's own people. If God's elect people are held to such a high standard (compare Amos 3:2), should

131

not the rest of the world also pay attention to "the word of the Lord" (Micah 1:1)?

Yes, all the world should pay close attention because the Lord comes as both Witness and Judge (compare Malachi 3:5). Furthermore, when God arrives, the world cannot remain unaffected (Micah 1:3–4). The transcendent, holy God will come from "his place" beyond human knowledge or control and will encounter all creation with irresistible power. God's arrival is like a volcanic eruption, an earthquake that registers "10" on the Richter scale, and a devastating flood all rolled together. If the most permanent features of the earth's surface cannot escape unscathed in God's presence, how can sinful people hope to withstand God's coming? Let all the world learn that it is impossible to oppose God, the Righteous Judge.

> If greed is expressed in the words, "I want things," then covetousness is expressed in the words, "I want your things."

## Samaria's Sin (1:6–7)

Micah may have carried out a long period of ministry to the Northern Kingdom if he began preaching at the very beginning of Jotham's reign in 742 BC. It is more probable that his proclamation started closer to the fall of Samaria around 722 BC. Whatever preaching mission to Israel this Judean prophet may have had, the announcement of judgment in 1:6–7 is the only oracle of Micah that is directed specifically to Samaria. It represents all of his preaching to the North, and its very form testifies to the failure of Micah's hearers to heed his message. The Lord announced the ruin of the city.

# Covet

Just as the English language has several words that express the emotion of wanting what belongs to another (for example, *desire, crave, covet*), the Hebrew language also has various terms for the concept of coveting. The word *chamad* denotes the emotion of desire and often also the accompanying activity of obtaining. Significantly, the word that Micah used in 2:1 is *chamad*.

It should be noted that *chamad* does not always appear in a negative context. In Psalm 19:10 the ordinances of the Lord are to be desired (*chamad*). Even today sometimes we hear someone say, "I covet your prayers."

The charges against the Northern Kingdom are not explicitly described like those against Judah will be in chapter 2. Instead, we see that the reason for God's punishment lies in the religious unfaithfulness of God's people. Verse 7 speaks of what will happen to the images and idols of the city. Idolatry is the reason that God would treat Samaria, his people, as his enemy. Micah described the people's worship of Baal as prostitution (1:7). Perhaps the punishment announced in this verse means that the very idols of Israel would be carried to Assyria as plunder, or perhaps that the idols of Israel's spiritual prostitution would be melted down by individual Assyrian soldiers and used for procuring prostitutes for themselves.

## The Judging of Judah (1:8–16)

The lament over Judah that begins in 1:8 marks a transition in the Book of Micah. This passage came up to twenty years after the fall of Samaria, sometime prior to Sennacherib's invasion of Judah in 701 BC. Micah recognized the continuity between Samaria's wound and Judah's impending disaster (1:9). Verse 8 introduces Micah's words to Judah as a lament, a mourning song for the dead, as if the nation itself was as good as dead.

The lament itself (1:10–16) is an imaginative announcement of God's coming punishment. The lament plays on the meaning or sound of the names of various Judean cities that lie in Assyria's path. In our context, it is as if Micah were to say, *Stand in awe, Richmond, for what the Lord is going to do. Dallas will become worthless. Wolves will prowl in Houston and Atlanta. How the people will lament in Orlando. The Mississippi River will become Dry Gulch, and every populated city will become a ghost town whose only inhabitant is the tumbleweed.*

## Bold Thieves (2:1–5)

The funeral motif continues in this passage with the "Alas" of verse 1 and the lament of verse 4. The lamentation "Alas for" (2:1) is usually followed by the name of the deceased, but here it is followed by a description of those who are under God's death sentence. They spend all night planning evil and then carry out their plans bright and early the next morning. These evil plans, according to verse 2, include oppressing people and taking away their houses and land. These evildoers are no ordinary thieves, however. The normal thief spends the daytime planning a heist and uses the cover of darkness to carry it out. That those condemned by Micah could carry out their plans in broad daylight suggests that these are powerful people and that their evil deeds may also be legal acts. How well we know that legal and moral are not necessarily the same thing!

The last phrase of verse 1 has a clear meaning. These evildoers have the power to accomplish what they plan. A more literal translation of the word "power" is *hand*. *Hand* in Hebrew is often symbolic of power. Some early Jewish interpreters preferred to see the Hebrew word for "power" as the same word for God. Their understanding of the phrase was that the evildoers did this because they did not lift their hands to God. This explains their motivation (a lack of religious feeling) more than their ability. Another way to read the phrase would be to understand the reference in the Hebrew to *hand* as *fist*. Thus the translation could be, *For their fist is their God.* Thus the idea would be that might is right.[1]

> *Micah's voice . . . still speaks clearly to our generation in which the desire for things is as strong as ever.*

The remaining question is this: How could these people take houses and fields away from their rightful owners in broad daylight? There is no evidence that these were marauding bands who took possession of properties by force of violence. Perhaps the powerful ones are government officials or military leaders sent from Jerusalem to bolster the outlying defenses around the capital. They took advantage of their positions to confiscate property for themselves in the name of "national security." A more likely explanation is that the powerful ones were rich people who made loans to the poorer farmers and then foreclosed on the loans when the borrower could not repay. Our day is not the first time lenders make high interest loans to those least able to pay them back. We have even seen how some real estate agents and realty lawyers take advantage of inheritance laws to get property at unfairly low prices when people die without a will. Such activity, even if it is legal, would be roundly condemned by the prophet as unjust oppression.

> *Could it be that we ourselves are guilty of the sin of covetousness?*

Land and family are uniquely protected in the Old Testament. From the time of the settlement of the Promised Land under Joshua, each family had been given an inheritance, a plot of land that should be for that family in perpetuity. Land was divided evenly among the broader population.

Even when property was sold, the transaction was not permanent, but in the year of Jubilee would revert to its original family as that family's inalienable inheritance. Such practice was to guarantee the basic equality of all citizens of the Holy Land, rather than the establishment of a wealthy, elite class. It was not until the eighth century BC, when great prosperity came to some, that the concept of large

*How well we know that legal and moral are not necessarily the same thing!*

estates arose in Israel and Judah. Any attempt to establish large estates, however, had to ignore God's word and would be detrimental to maintaining a sense of community among the people of God.

A life devoted to the use of wealth and power makes the sin of covetousness even more dangerous. The powerful saw something as advantageous or desirable and felt they could give their mind unreservedly not only to devising ways of taking possession of the thing, but also to anticipating the enjoyment of that possession. They could not imagine anything that would prevent them from doing so. Their "desire for" led irrevocably to taking.

The prophet, however, announced that God was not unresponsive to such oppression. The oppressors themselves would soon be lifting up their voices in laments. They would lose what they had taken, and more (2:4). The punishment that God announced here is similar to that found in Isaiah 5:8. In both cases, the ones who had taken over property would find themselves alone, defenseless, and ultimately conquered by the Assyrians. If the powerful drove out all others, they would have no others to help them. They would have to endure the taunt songs of the invaders.

Thus, any appeal to the religious community about property would be the height of hypocrisy. No one, not even God, would listen to it.

## A Free Pulpit? (2:6–7a)

Micah's audience refused to listen any longer. They objected to his message, calling for him to stop preaching because economics was not a proper subject for preaching. They felt insulted and asked whether the situation was really that bad.

They asked questions like these (2:7): *Does God ever run out of patience? Would a loving God really punish his people like this?* They felt the prophet was wrong. They began to criticize Micah's sermons and theology.

# Is Gambling Covetousness?

There is a difference between taking a risk and gambling. One takes a risk by opening a business but hopes to make a profit by providing a service to paying clients. Gambling, on the other hand, is trying to make a profit without providing a service but rather by taking the money that belongs to others.

Does this definition make gambling an activity of covetousness? How should one classify playing the lottery? Is investing in the stock market gambling or risk taking? Is it coveting?

## The Prophet's Defense (2:7b–9)

Micah answered his critics' questions with a rhetorical question from God (2:7b): "Do not my words do good to one who walks uprightly?" Note the phrase "one who walks uprightly." The contrast is seen in verse 8: "But you . . . ."

The destructive power of coveting is shown, and it goes far beyond the loss of property. Coveting had destroyed community. Those who had oppressed others had treated their brothers and sisters as enemies. These evildoers had left their fellow members of the family of God without even the security of a cloak, which was specifically protected by law (Exodus 22:26–27). Stripped like prisoners of war and driven out like refugees, the most vulnerable of the family of God suffered because of the covetousness and greed of the powerful. Those who wanted only to live peacefully had been ravaged by war even before the Assyrians arrived. Now God would use the Assyrian army to punish the evildoers.

> *Coveting had destroyed community.*

## What About Us?

Yes, what about us? Applying these Scriptures to our day, our society, and our lives calls for painful honesty. Could it be that we ourselves are guilty of the sin of covetousness? Could it be that our acts of covetousness, which we may consider small though wrong, are causing great hurt to our society, especially to the most vulnerable people?

Could it be that we, too, are liable to God's judgment? "Do not be deceived; God is not mocked, for you reap whatever you sow" (Galatians 6:7).

## QUESTIONS

1. Coveting leads to the loss of far more than simply things.
   How does the community suffer where coveting is evident?
   How do individuals suffer? What loss does the one who covets suffer?

2. Does coveting always lead to taking? Is there anything wrong with just a little "greedy daydreaming"?

3. Does our society as a whole encourage and practice coveting? Is there any evidence that our coveting is under God's judgment?

4. What help can the church offer to people in dealing with greed and coveting?

## NOTES

1. William McKane, *The Book of Micah* (Edinburgh: T & T Clark, 1998), 60.

## Focal Text
Micah 3

## Background
Micah 3

## Main Idea
God holds leaders accountable for behaving justly and leading people in the right way.

## Question to Explore
What leadership qualities do you value?

## Study Aim
To decide to exercise the leadership traits God blesses and encourage these traits in leaders I support

## Study and Action Emphases
- Affirm the Bible as our authoritative guide for life and ministry
- Develop a growing, vibrant faith
- Value all people as created in the image of God
- Obey and serve Jesus by meeting physical, spiritual, and emotional needs
- Equip people for servant leadership

# LESSON TWELVE

# When Leaders Sell Out

## Quick Read

God desires leaders who care for others more than for self. There is no place for those who would abuse others in order to gain personal success. God wants leaders of courage and integrity who depend on the Holy Spirit for guidance. The abuse of power and unrestrained greed result in disaster for both leaders and followers.

The grandmother of philosopher and preacher Howard Thurmond was an ex-slave who never learned to read. She often had her grandson read the Bible to her. She loved the gospels and the psalms, but she never wanted to hear the epistles of Paul (unless it was an occasional reading of 1 Corinthians 13).

When asked about her selectivity in Scripture, she explained that when she was a slave her master would not allow the Negro preacher to address the slaves. Instead, the master personally chose a white preacher. The white preacher always selected a passage by Paul, and his favorite was Ephesians 6:5: "Slaves, obey your earthly masters with fear and trembling, in singleness of heart, as you obey Christ." The sermon would be a demonstration that slavery was a part of God's will, and that the slaves would be blessed by God if they were good slaves. Thurmond's grandmother made a vow to God that if she were ever freed and learned to read, she would never read that part of the Bible again. Although she never learned to read, she kept her promise by refusing to have the epistles read in her presence. She had been a victim of the use of religious teaching as a means of oppression, and she wanted no more of it.[1] Micah would have understood and would have been her advocate.

# Micah 3

1 And I said:
Listen, you heads of Jacob
and rulers of the house of Israel!
Should you not know justice?—
2 you who hate the good and love the evil,
who tear the skin off my people,
and the flesh off their bones;
3 who eat the flesh of my people,
flay their skin off them,
break their bones in pieces,
and chop them up like meat in a kettle,
like flesh in a caldron.
4 Then they will cry to the LORD,
but he will not answer them;
he will hide his face from them at that time,
because they have acted wickedly.
5 Thus says the LORD concerning the prophets

who lead my people astray,
who cry "Peace"
when they have something to eat,
but declare war against those
who put nothing into their mouths.
6 Therefore it shall be night to you, without vision,
and darkness to you, without revelation.
The sun shall go down upon the prophets,
and the day shall be black over them;
7 the seers shall be disgraced,
and the diviners put to shame;
they shall all cover their lips,
for there is no answer from God.
8 But as for me, I am filled with power,
with the spirit of the LORD,
and with justice and might,
to declare to Jacob his transgression
and to Israel his sin.
9 Hear this, you rulers of the house of Jacob
and chiefs of the house of Israel,
who abhor justice
and pervert all equity,
10 who build Zion with blood
and Jerusalem with wrong!
11 Its rulers give judgment for a bribe,
its priests teach for a price,
its prophets give oracles for money;
yet they lean upon the LORD and say,
"Surely the LORD is with us!
No harm shall come upon us."
12 Therefore because of you
Zion shall be plowed as a field;
Jerusalem shall become a heap of ruins,
and the mountain of the house a wooded height.

## Cannibals for Leaders (3:1–4)

In this passage Micah addressed the "heads" and "rulers" of Judah (3:1).
That the names "Jacob" and "house of Israel" (3:1, 9) describe Judah can
be seen by reading 3:9–10. There the rulers and chiefs of Jacob and the

house of Israel are described as building "Zion" and "Jerusalem," the capital of Judah. The reference to Judah is also indicated by the words "And I said" at the beginning of 3:1, which serve to tie chapter 3 to chapter 2, words that address Judah. In fact, the Northern Kingdom of Israel had ceased to exist some twenty years before Micah proclaimed these words. Judah was all that was left of David's Israel, of Jacob's heritage. Now the leaders, these "heads" and "rulers," were putting the whole nation of Judah in danger.

The first words of chapter 3, "And I said," indicate that Micah is speaking for himself. It is an unusual manner in which to begin a section, and

*. . . The leaders . . . were putting the whole nation of Judah in danger.*

many scholars have wondered whether there was once a narrative context for these events, which we no longer have. Perhaps we can imagine a fitting setting. It is possible that Micah's preaching recorded in chapter 2 caused such a big stir in the towns around Jerusalem that a civil and military council or tribunal was formed to investigate the accusations that had been made against the prophet. Appearing as a witness before this judicial committee, Micah boldly used the occasion to accuse them of misleading the people.

Micah incredulously asked those responsible for justice (3:1), "Should you not know justice?" He was doing more than asking, *Shouldn't you know what the law says?* The Hebrew word translated "know" is one of intimate experience, not intellectual acquaintance (see Genesis 4:1). The rhetorical question was really an accusation that these leaders had no personal experience or deeply felt commitment to the practice of justice. Instead, Micah declared, they "hate the good and love the evil" (3:2).

The distinction between what is good and what is evil is at the very heart of justice. Isaiah urged the people of God, "Cease to do evil, learn to do good" (Isaiah 1:16b–17a). Amos declared that the way to establish justice is to "hate evil and love good" (Amos 5:15a). The word pair *love/hate* in Hebrew includes more than the emotions we understand in English. It is a common way in the Old Testament to declare a deeply held personal preference for, acceptance of, and disposition toward one thing in opposition to another. These civil and military leaders had demonstrated by their actions a personal preference for evil.

Micah described those actions by means of a gruesome, emotional metaphor (Micah 3:2b–3). The leaders were like cannibals butchering their own people.

Micah declared that the leaders who were most responsible for protecting the "little people" were guilty of exploiting them for personal gain. Not only would this refer to seizing personal property through manipulating economic policies and the legal system, but also to these government officials' using the forced labor of common citizens.

Such an abuse of power on the part of the leaders indicates that they had no regard for God's law about caring for the less fortunate. They did not respond to the cry of the poor; in fact, they were the ones making the poor cry out! Therefore, when these leaders found themselves in a desperate situation and cried out to God, the Lord was not going to respond to them. When these leaders turned to God for protection in the time of danger that was coming, the Lord would "hide his face from them" (3:4). That is, the Lord would remove his active presence from them. Without God's presence and help, they had no hope of survival. The punishment would fit the crime.

> *Avarice can never be a leadership trait among God's people, and justice can never be sold to the highest bidder.*

# Fulfillment of Prophecy

If Micah expected Jerusalem to be destroyed by the Assyrians, he was wrong. Sennacherib did attack Judah, but Jerusalem did not fall. Instead, God preserved Zion by a miracle (see Isaiah 36—37 and 2 Kings 18:13–19:37). The lack of fulfillment of Micah's prophecy certainly did not do much for Micah's immediate acceptance as a true prophet. He was not, however, forgotten.

A century or so later, when Jeremiah preached a sermon also announcing the destruction of Jerusalem and the temple, some wanted to kill him. Jeremiah's life was preserved when others recalled the preaching of Micah of Moresheth (Jeremiah 26:1–19).

The elders there took into account that all prophecy is conditional. Micah preached judgment. Hezekiah, however, turned to the Lord, and the Lord relented. Not every prediction of the Old Testament prophets has a literal fulfillment, but that does not deny the authenticity of their words. As people respond, God may alter his plan, or the fulfillment of the prophetic word may be accomplished in a way unforeseen by the prophet. Furthermore, Micah's announcement of judgment against Jerusalem did come true some one hundred or so years later when Judah refused to turn to the Lord in the face of the Babylonian threat.

## Left in the Dark (3:5–8)

Micah turned his attention to the professional, court prophets. Their behavior as the religious leaders of God's people was just as destructive to the community as were the actions of the "heads" and "rulers." This is not just Micah sharing his own opinions, but "Thus says the Lord" (3:5).

The complaint that God had against these prophets was that they "lead my people astray" (3:5). The Hebrew word translated "lead . . . astray" certainly means *to cause to wander, to make one lose the way*, but it may also refer to the staggering, lurching walk of a drunkard, *to make one stagger about aimlessly*. The charge may be that of introducing aimless confusion as much as an intentional misleading into error. The prophets so misled the people that the people did not know right from wrong. They had so confused the people that, even if the people were to choose the right way, they could not walk straight down the path.

In the second half of verse 5, Micah clarified how the professional prophets led the people astray. He did not say that these prophets had not received any word from God. Instead, the problem lay in the way that they had shared that word with others. The prophets had preached for profit! They gave the word of "peace" (*shalom*), of wholeness and salvation, to those who gave them something to eat. On the other hand, these religious leaders declared war against those who "put nothing into their mouths" (3:5) That is, they expressed their personal hostility toward the person with a message of doom. The language of feeding the prophet probably stems from the fact that the earliest seers/prophets depended upon "presents" of food for their livelihood (see 1 Samuel 9:7; 1 Kings 14:2–3). Nevertheless, what is meant here is not a living wage, but a bribe. The difference between a prophetic blessing or curse depended on the amount of money received for the service. For these prophets, it was money, not God, that talked. It is no accident, then, that Micah used the Hebrew word meaning *to bite* rather than the word meaning *to eat*. It is the regular word for a snakebite. Even when the message is *shalom*—peace and prosperity—it cannot be trusted. The words of these false prophets had a lethal effect on the people of Judah.

*We must allow Micah's words to challenge the way we behave as church members.*

Once again, the punishment fits the crime. Micah offered a long, detailed announcement of judgment on these deceptive "prophets"/"seers"/"diviners" (3:6–7). The three titles are somewhat synonymous designations for the false prophets. The first is the general word for prophet in the Old Testament. The second, "seer," probably refers to the way prophetic figures often received revelation from God, by means of a vision. The third term, "diviner," identifies the person that receives revelation by the reading of omens. The Old Testament used this word to speak of foreign prophetic-like characters (see Deuteronomy 18:14) or as a pejorative term for an Israelite prophet. Micah thus used two words that were perfectly good designations of prophets but added the third term to describe his opponents. In this way, Micah designated them as false prophets. Whatever may have been their good beginning was coming to an end; darkness would overtake them. There would be no revelation or vision; these false prophets would be left without a word from God. They would have to shut their mouths in shame and disgrace. They would be left lost and confused, staggering and stumbling in the dark, just as they had left the nation lost and confused by their mishandling the word of the Lord.

*The reason for all this, Micah emphatically said to the leaders he addressed, is you!*

In contrast to the false prophets, Micah described himself as a true prophet (3:8). What are we to make of this verse that seems like boasting? The prophet's description of himself, however, was not like Little Jack Horner saying, "What a good boy am I." Rather, Micah spoke these words to identify what was lacking in the lives of his prophetic opponents. Micah was not making great claims in and of himself. Notice he said that he was "filled," filled to overflowing. What power Micah had was God's power. The Spirit of God filled him with courage, and thus the bravery that Micah exhibited was a gift. Micah did not claim himself as its source. Even his sense of justice was more than a keen conscience. It was God's gift of the ability to discern the difference between good and evil, between that which builds community and that which destroys it. God had called Micah and equipped him to do what no one else wanted to do, to announce firmly the sin of the whole of God's people and its awful consequences.

## Leading Only to Disaster (3:9–12)

Once again Micah turned to the military and civil leaders of Judah, the same group addressed in 3:1 as indicated by the use of the same Hebrew

# Case Study

A county known for its growing affluence presented a dilemma to its churches. The land that held a trailer park was sold by its out-of-state owner to a nationally-known commercial enterprise. That business wanted to build a new store and offered a $2,000 moving assistance check to the park's residents, many of whom had lived there for more than fifteen years at a near-poverty level.

The county board of supervisors approved the business venture, but they refused to take action that would have allowed the creation of another trailer park in the county. Furthermore, many residents found that their mobile homes were in too poor a condition to be transported.

What are some things the churches could do to address the needs of the park residents? Are there other issues in this situation that the churches should address? What are they, and how would you proceed?

words. Micah's charge concerning their basic attitude was that they "abhor justice" and "pervert all equity" (3:9). This attitude led to actions that are again summarized in a gruesome metaphor (3:10). They "build Zion with blood and Jerusalem with wrong" (3:10). The Hebrew word translated "wrong" refers to a wrongful violence that can include murder.

> Amazingly, these leaders saw nothing wrong with their devotion to prosperity.

This speech of Micah does more than repeat his first confrontation with Judah's leadership. In verse 11 Micah condensed his charges against these leaders and the charges he had brought against the religious leaders (now including the temple priests as well as the court prophets) into one single accusation: greed. Each group based the performance of its task upon a "bribe," "price," or "money."

Micah was not complaining that these people got paid for their work. Certainly all should receive a fair salary for their livelihood. Micah, though, was condemning the fact that for these civil and religious "servants," the outcome of their service depended on the income they received. Gifts given in secret determined the outcome of lawsuits. The size of the offering affected the content of the religious instruction. The amount received controlled the direction of counseling.

Avarice can never be a leadership trait among God's people, and justice can never be sold to the highest bidder. Jesus said, "'You cannot serve God and wealth'" (Luke 16:13).

Amazingly, these leaders saw nothing wrong with their devotion to prosperity. If anything, the bigger budgets proved that God was on their side! Was it an outrageous cynicism or an incredible insensitivity to the contradiction of a dedication to prosperity and a dedication to God that allowed them to proclaim, "Surely the Lord is with us" (3:11)?

They confidently declared that no harm would come Jerusalem's way. They based this assurance on a theological idea that Jerusalem was the city of God and therefore would be protected no matter what (see Psalm 46:1–7; 48:1–8; Jeremiah 7:4). Micah could not disagree more! He declared that Zion/Jerusalem would be destroyed (Micah 3:12). The Holy City would become a place where crops were grown among piled ruins of stones. The temple mount would revert to a forest-covered hill.

*She had been a victim of the use of religious teaching as a means of oppression, and she wanted no more of it.*

*The reason for all this*, Micah emphatically said to the leaders he addressed, *is you*! If Micah was appearing before a council to review his preaching, one cannot imagine a more bold, climactic, or abrupt ending than that.

## The Relevance of the Word

Certainly we want our political, military, legal, and economic leaders to be people of integrity and justice. We do not want their deliberations clouded by greed or their decisions determined only by the bottom line. There is much they could learn from Micah. Nevertheless, we would do well to recognize that Micah's message is directed first to the community of faith, especially to the leaders of those claiming to be God's people, the church.

We must allow Micah's words to challenge the way we behave as church members. Are our churches captivated by wealth and success? Does a reading of this chapter give us pause when we would evaluate a church's health on the basis of the numbers involved in attendance and budget, or when we would model the pastoral role after the behavior of a CEO of a large corporation? In the larger world, do we as Christians close our eyes to instances of official injustice or even participate in it?

## QUESTIONS

1. What might be the five worst traits that a Christian leader could possess? What would you say are the five most desirable characteristics of a Christian leader?

2. What are some indications that a church has unhealthy attitudes about wealth?

3. If you were teaching a class of aspiring ministers, what would you tell them about the meaning and the limits of pastoral authority?

4. If you were praying that the Holy Spirit would fill your life with a certain attribute, what would be your priority request?

## NOTES

1. Renita J. Weems, *Listening for God* (New York: Simon & Schuster, 2000), 85–86.

## Focal Text

Micah 4:1–8; 5:2–5a

## Background

Micah 4—5

## Main Idea

God will provide peace to people who respond in faithfulness to him.

## Question to Explore

Is peace really possible?

## Study Aim

To describe the peace God provides and commit myself to live in faithfulness to God

### Study and Action Emphases

- Affirm the Bible as our authoritative guide for life and ministry
- Share the gospel with all people
- Develop a growing, vibrant faith
- Value all people as created in the image of God
- Obey and serve Jesus by meeting physical, spiritual, and emotional needs

# LESSON THIRTEEN

# Peace Is Coming

## Quick Read

God wants a relationship of peace and well-being with his people. God expects the people of God to be obedient to his way. The benefits of God's peace are to become realities in both time and eternity.

My wife and I recently made our first visit to Appomattox Court House in Virginia. The Civil War was officially ended there in 1865. It was quite an experience to stand where the most tragic war in our country's history came to an end. I was struck by the emphasis the National Park Service placed on the events at Appomattox. It was not a monument to the victory of one side or a memorial to the defeat of another. The message of each presentation was that of a peace that offered a chance for healing and reconciliation, rest and a sense of wholeness, to a nation torn and weary of war.

Perhaps the experience was so moving because America's "war against terrorism" still captures headlines. Who knows what the headlines will be when you read this lesson? In such a situation as the present, Micah's words about peace can sound like a dream—wonderful, idyllic, but impractical.

The visit to Appomattox made the possibility seem more real of men laying down their arms and returning to their homes, no longer using their horses as tools of war, but as instruments for farming. In our lesson, Micah offers to all of God's people the hope of an even greater peace that establishes our healing, wholeness, and total well-being in God.

# Micah 4:1–8

1 In days to come
the mountain of the LORD's house
shall be established as the highest of the mountains,
and shall be raised up above the hills.
Peoples shall stream to it,
2 and many nations shall come and say:
"Come, let us go up to the mountain of the LORD,
to the house of the God of Jacob;
that he may teach us his ways
and that we may walk in his paths."
For out of Zion shall go forth instruction,
and the word of the LORD from Jerusalem.
3 He shall judge between many peoples,
and shall arbitrate between strong nations far away;
they shall beat their swords into plowshares,
and their spears into pruning hooks;
nation shall not lift up sword against nation,
neither shall they learn war any more;

⁴ but they shall all sit under their own vines and under their own fig
    trees,
  and no one shall make them afraid;
  for the mouth of the LORD of hosts has spoken.
⁵ For all the peoples walk,
  each in the name of its god,
  but we will walk in the name of the LORD our God
  forever and ever.
⁶ In that day, says the LORD,
  I will assemble the lame
  and gather those who have been driven away,
  and those whom I have afflicted.
⁷ The lame I will make the remnant,
  and those who were cast off, a strong nation;
  and the LORD will reign over them in Mount Zion
  now and forevermore.
⁸ And you, O tower of the flock,
  hill of daughter Zion,
  to you it shall come,
  the former dominion shall come,
  the sovereignty of daughter Jerusalem.

# Micah 5:2–5a

² But you, O Bethlehem of Ephrathah,
  who are one of the little clans of Judah,
  from you shall come forth for me
  one who is to rule in Israel,
  whose origin is from of old,
  from ancient days.
³ Therefore he shall give them up until the time
  when she who is in labor has brought forth;
  then the rest of his kindred shall return
  to the people of Israel.
⁴ And he shall stand and feed his flock in the strength of the LORD,
  in the majesty of the name of the LORD his God.
  And they shall live secure, for now he shall be great
  to the ends of the earth;
⁵ and he shall be the one of peace.

## Is Judgment God's Final Word? (4:1–7)

Micah 4:1–4 stands in marked contrast to the grim words of Micah 3:12. The message in 4:1–4 is, *the beginning*, whereas 3:12 cries out, *the end*. It is not necessary to suppose that chapter 4 begins with a later addition to the book by a different author, as some suggest. The Book of Hosea offers a striking similarity (compare Hosea 1:2–9 with Hosea 1:10–11). It seems more likely that these eighth-century prophets purposefully placed judgment and salvation oracles side by side to map out the alternatives facing the people of God. If the fulfillment of prophetic proclamation is conditional, based on the response of the people to the message, then the prophets wanted to clarify the options for the people by placing them together.

*Micah offers to all of God's people the hope of an even greater peace that establishes our healing, wholeness, and total well-being in God.*

God does not want judgment to be the last word. God offers salvation as the final word, if people will only choose to repent from their ways and walk in God's paths.

Micah expressed such a hope to the people of Judah, just as Hosea had done earlier for the Northern Kingdom, Israel.

Micah 4:1–3 shares a striking similarity in content with another eighth-century prophet, Isaiah (compare Isaiah 2:2–4 with Micah 4:1–3). Isaiah does not contain the description of the good life as seen from the perspective of a farmer in the Judean countryside (Micah 4:4), but everything else

# Shalom

The Hebrew word normally translated "peace" is *shalom*. It comes from the verb meaning "to be whole" or "to be complete." *Shalom* certainly does mean peace in the sense of an absence of conflict and war. Its meaning, however, goes far beyond just the cessation of fighting. *Shalom* includes the idea that after the fighting has stopped, what has been broken is made whole. Wounds are healed and relationships are restored.

The emphasis of prophets such as Micah, Isaiah, Jonah, and Zechariah is on the possibility of peace that results in reconciliation and friendship, in the well-being of all because of a mutual trust in God. This element of trust in God to provide peace gave rise to the non-violent attitude of the New Testament martyrs. If one is at peace with God, accepting God's gift of wholeness and well-being (salvation), then life or death can be faced with confidence, and there is no need for fear.

is almost identical. What few differences exist are so minor, such as in the word order of "nations" and "peoples," that some literary dependence must exist (compare Micah 4:3 and Isaiah 2:4). It is impossible, however, to determine whether Micah used Isaiah's material or Isaiah used that of Micah. It is certainly possible (and perhaps more likely) that both prophets were drawing on existing material that was held in common within the prophetic traditions of Judah. (See also the brief article, "Micah 4:1–3; Isaiah 2:2–4; Joel 3:9–10.")

Micah's (and Isaiah's) vision of God's salvation is remarkable because of its inclusiveness. God's instruction and guidance would not be available only to Israel, but to "many nations" (4:2) and "many peoples" (4:3). This would take place "in days to come" (4:1). This phrase referring to the future is more literally *in the days behind*. We talk of the future as something that lies ahead and consider ourselves as moving forward toward it, as if we were paddling a canoe. The Hebrew mind understood the journey into the future as if we were rowing a rowboat. Where we are going is to our backs. Thus it is unseen, unknown, yet to be revealed.

In that future day that God was revealing, "the mountain of the Lord's house" would dominate the landscape. Far from being overgrown ruins (3:12), the temple would become the focus of the pilgrimage of an international flood of peoples. They were not coming as conquering armies but as willing students of God's word (4:2). Jerusalem would be the source of "instruction" for all the world. The reference is to God's own "instruction" about how to live honestly, justly, and peacefully in specific life situations. God would be fulfilling the role as King, judging and arbitrating with complete wisdom and justice all misunderstandings and conflicts so there would be no need of war. Instead, the resources of the world could be transformed into agricultural tools that provide life, not gobbled up in an arms race that brings death. Instead of fearing destruction by enemy armies or confiscation by covetous officials, each person would live securely with what is sufficient for a good life. According to Micah, this is a divine promise: "the mouth of the Lord of hosts has spoken" (4:4).

*God offers salvation as the final word, if people will only choose to repent from their ways and walk in God's paths.*

Micah's vision of peace occurs within the realm of history. Micah does not say that peace will arrive "when we all get to heaven." Rather, peace is a real possibility, an attainable goal for life here on earth. If humanity would willingly order life according to God's instruction, peace would become a reality. With the grace of God and the faithfulness of God's people, such a time is a real possibility.

Not everyone agreed with Micah. If Micah 2:6–7a records the objections of Micah's opponents to his words of judgment, then Micah 4:5 may record their objection to Micah's word of a salvation and peace that includes all "peoples." Micah's opponents refused to believe that the present situation of conflicting peoples and conflicting gods could change. *No!* they cried. *The other peoples will always follow their false gods and idols. We and we alone, though, will be faithful to the true God, and our faithfulness will be forever. Things will never change. Salvation is for us, not them.* Those opposed to Micah saw no possibility for a mutually shared peace on earth.

> *The Hebrew mind understood the journey into the future as if we were rowing a rowboat.*

Verses 6–7 are Micah's answer to his critics. His opponents' speech had been filled with self-assurance and belief in their own strength. Notice their emphatic use of the pronoun "we" and the emphasis on their own faithful works (4:5b). In contrast, in 4:2–3 everything depended on the gracious activity of the Lord ("he"). Once again, Micah points out that salvation is given by the Lord alone (notice the pronoun "I" in 4:6–7).

Rather than assume Israel's self-sufficiency and strength, Micah points out the weakness of those who will find God's peace. They are the outcast, the wounded, and the lame. Micah leaves their point of origin vague. They may be from among any with whom the Lord has been dealing in judgment ("whom I have afflicted," 4:6). Therefore, they may not come from only one nation, but they will be formed into "a strong nation" (4:7), that is, into God's "remnant," those under his rule forever.

## The Dialogue Continues (4:8—5:1)

The dialogue between opposing viewpoints continues in Micah 4:8—5:1, but it may not be possible to identify with certainty who was carrying on the conversation. Is this the record of the exchange between Micah and his opponents, or is it a collection of voices that entered the discussion more than a century later, at the time of the destruction of Jerusalem and later in the Exile? The presence of 4:10 with its statement of exile in Babylon and the restoration of Israel at least suggests the latter.

# A Teachable Moment?

Suppose your eight-year-old child has had a confrontation with an eight-year-old playmate. Your child was called names. Ugly words and a few shoves were exchanged. The other child was clearly in the wrong and instigated the incident.

What are the options your daughter has in regard to her relationship with this playmate? Is there something you can do to teach your daughter about how and why to be a peacemaker? Do you think you could get over *your* anger and protective feelings to help your daughter become a peacemaker?

Whatever the case, whether 4:8—5:1 is a collection of eighth-century conversations, fifth-century conversations, "updated" versions of eighth-century conversations, or some combination of all three, the important point is that in these verses, under God's guidance, a debate about the future of God's people is heard. This debate continues to this day.

Micah 4:8 affirms that God's people will have a role to play in the coming future. This verse is expressed from the perspective that Jerusalem has suffered defeat and that thus flocks of sheep inhabit the hill upon which the city had been built. An opposing voice speaks in 4:9: *Why do you act like Jerusalem has lost its leaders and suffered pains? That is not going to happen.* The prophetic voice speaks again in 4:10–11, adopting the image of labor pains the opposition had introduced, saying, *Yes, in fact it will be just like labor. You are going to hurt because you will be taken away from Jerusalem into Babylon. But*

> If humanity would willingly order life according to God's instruction, peace would become a reality.

*like childbirth, pain is not the end. The Lord will redeem you. It is true that now the nations are against you, intent on their victory. But they do not know the Lord's purpose in all of this. God has gathered them like sheaves; God's harvest will include all the nations.*

## A Different Kind of Messiah (5:2–5a)

At the very darkest moment for the people of Judah, God gave the promise of a saving ruler who would bring them security and peace. This ruler would come from the clan of Ephrathah in the town of Bethlehem, a small, militarily insignificant place a few miles south of Jerusalem. These

# Micah 4:1–3; Isaiah 2:2–4; Joel 3:9–10

An evaluation of Micah 4:1–3 and Isaiah 2:2–4 becomes even more complicated when one considers Joel 3:9–10, which reads: "Proclaim this among the nations: / Prepare war, / stir up the warriors. / Let all the soldiers draw near, / let them come up. / Beat your plowshares into swords, / and your pruning hooks into spears; / let the weakling say, 'I am a warrior.'"

Some scholars hold that the Book of Joel was written before Isaiah or Micah. If this is true, then Isaiah and Micah would be reversing a call to arms in a battle between the nations and Israel's God so that instead God offers a call to peace to all the nations.

As attractive as such a view might be, it seems more likely that Joel was a later prophet who intentionally parodied the message of Micah and Isaiah so that there was an ironic (almost sarcastic) call to the enemies of God to find and arm as many people as they could in their final, futile, apocalyptic battle against the Lord. This call certainly is a completely opposite alternative to the more universal vision found in Micah and Isaiah.

---

words recall the origins of Israel's greatest king, David. The emphasis, though, is not on David seated on a throne in Jerusalem ruling over an empire he had conquered. Rather the emphasis is on David the shepherd boy of Bethlehem, the youngest of eight brothers (1 Samuel 16:1–13). This ruler would act as a shepherd (Micah 5:4).

The prophet understood that this deliverer would not appear until after the defeat of Jerusalem and Judah's experience of exile (5:3).

*God's gift of peace through Jesus Christ affects both this world and the world to come.*

Nevertheless, with the image of childbirth, the prophet transformed this defeat at the hands of God into something more than mere punishment. God was offering a future to his people. They would experience the rule of the Shepherd Ruler who is "the one of peace" (5:5a). He would "feed" (5:4; literally, "shepherd," that is, nourish, guide and protect) all his flock. The flock would "live" in security (5:4). Too, the Shepherd's flock would extend "to the ends of the earth" (5:4).

The promise of the Shepherd Ruler (5:2–5a) is similar to the vision of peace found in 4:1–4. The rule of the Shepherd would be peaceful and universal. It would not depend on the strength of human armies or the majesty of a human court but would be wholly dependent on God.

Micah pleaded with his people to see this as God's plan and the destiny of God's people.

## The Fulfillment of Micah's Prophecy

History tells us that Judah experienced defeat, as Israel had a century-and-a-half before. Jerusalem was destroyed in 587 BC. The people went into exile. They were indeed rescued (see Micah 4:10; 5:3), but the people continued to debate whether God's people should be inclusive or exclusive until with Nehemiah the party of exclusion began to dominate Jewish life. The promise of a universal Shepherd Ruler who was Peace seemed unfulfilled. Then a baby was born in Bethlehem who was indeed the Prince of Peace and the Good Shepherd.

> *Peace will not come by means of weapons of destruction, but by surrender to the leadership of the Shepherd Ruler who is Peace.* Jesus!

Jesus Christ is the Messiah, and he is different from the kind of Messiah the Jews were expecting. We believe that Jesus is the Savior of the whole world, and his kingdom is open to any and all who respond to him in faith. He is the source of peace.

## Relevance for Today

We can no more dismiss these words of Micah than we can dismiss the words of Jesus, "Blessed are the peacemakers" (Matthew 5:9), by saying, *Of course, that means only spiritual peace.* God's gift of peace through Jesus Christ affects both this world and the world to come.

We are to be peacemakers at a personal level (Romans 12:18), as church members, and as citizens who can affect our nation's policies, as well as helping others to find the spiritual peace available to those who were once enemies of God (Rom. 5:10). Peace, wholeness, harmony, well-being and salvation are the business of God's people. Peace will not come by means of weapons of destruction, but by surrender to the leadership of the Shepherd Ruler who is Peace. Jesus!

## QUESTIONS

1. What are some things that happen in the church that cause conflict? How can an individual member help restore peace?

2. Is there such a thing as a "just war"? According to the major criteria that have been proposed by Christians through the centuries, a "just war" must meet these conditions: (a) have a just cause; (b) be declared by a legitimate authority; (c) have the goal of restoring peace; (d) have a reasonable chance of success; (e) use destruction in proportion to the wrong and to the intended benefits; (f) discriminate between civilians and soldiers and avoid doing harm to civilians; and (g) be engaged in as a last resort. Do you agree with these criteria? Why or why not? Would you add any other criteria?

3. What is the difference between trying to live in peace with all others and being a "doormat"?

## Focal Text
Micah 6:1–8

## Background
Micah 6—7

## Main Idea
In response to God's grace, we are to express our faithfulness to him by showing justice and kindness toward other people.

## Question to Explore
What does God want from you?

## Study Aim
To evaluate how I am fulfilling God's requirements and respond to God by showing justice and kindness toward other people

## Study and Action Emphases
- Affirm the Bible as our authoritative guide for life and ministry
- Share the gospel with all people
- Develop a growing, vibrant faith
- Value all people as created in the image of God
- Obey and serve Jesus by meeting physical, spiritual, and emotional needs
- Equip people for servant leadership

# LESSON FOURTEEN

# God's Case Against His People

## Quick Read
When nothing can be said against God, who has acted only out of love to build community with his people, the fault can only be with people. What can be done to restore the relationship? What God looks for is a teachable, loving commitment to put God's will into practice.

What does "to do justice, and to love kindness, and to walk humbly with your God" look like (Micah 6:8)? It sounds like such a tall order. Isn't that something that only law enforcement officers, diplomats, or great philanthropists can really accomplish?

Out of the despair of being unable to do anything great, we often fail to do anything at all. My wife Sandy has shown me how to move beyond such ethical paralysis. She pursues justice by volunteering at our local Ten Thousand Villages store. Ten Thousand Villages is a non-profit, Mennonite program through which quality handicrafts from around the world are sold and the artisans receive a fair price in a timely fashion for their work. The organization also monitors the working conditions of the artisan workers in their homeland to make sure that the conditions are just. Sandy's work as a volunteer helps ensure that otherwise unemployed, or underemployed, workers around the world have money to provide food, health care, and housing for their families.

Many people can speak of similar efforts to help provide justice for the poor through such organizations as Habitat for Humanity or through their service on a local housing or transportation commission. Yes, there is little recognition and no fanfare associated with these positions, but isn't that part of the "humble walk" in the first place?

# Micah 6:1–8

1 Hear what the LORD says:
Rise, plead your case before the mountains,
and let the hills hear your voice.
2 Hear, you mountains, the controversy of the LORD,
and you enduring foundations of the earth;
for the LORD has a controversy with his people,
and he will contend with Israel.
3 "O my people, what have I done to you?
In what have I wearied you? Answer me!
4 For I brought you up from the land of Egypt,
and redeemed you from the house of slavery;
and I sent before you Moses,
Aaron, and Miriam.
5 O my people, remember now what King Balak of Moab devised,
what Balaam son of Beor answered him,
and what happened from Shittim to Gilgal,
that you may know the saving acts of the LORD."

> 6 "With what shall I come before the LORD,
>   and bow myself before God on high?
>   Shall I come before him with burnt offerings,
>   with calves a year old? *Myself as a living Sacrifice*
> 7 Will the LORD be pleased with thousands of rams,
>   with ten thousands of rivers of oil?
>   Shall I give my firstborn for my transgression,
>   the fruit of my body for the sin of my soul?"
> 8 He has told you, O mortal, what is good;
>   and what does the LORD require of you
>   but to do justice, and to love kindness,
>   and to walk humbly with your God?

## A Day in Court (6:1–5)

Micah 6:1–2 includes three sets of imperatives—"Hear" (6:1a); "Rise, plead" (6:1b); and "Hear" (6:2). To interpret the passage well, we must discover who is being addressed in each set and why. Let's begin with the one that we know. Micah 6:2 is God's summons to the heights and depths of the earth to serve as witnesses to the litigation taking place between God and the people of God.

The "mountains" are to be the jury that hears the testimony offered in this covenant lawsuit. The mountains (6:1b; 6:2a; and the poetic synonym "hills" in 6:1b) had already been identified as such in Micah 6:1. The summons of 6:2 simply reveals more fully the depth of the jury pool. The "mountains" and the "foundations of the earth" are not disinterested parties. The whole earth, from top to bottom, has a stake in the human response to God. This is an important trial for all parties.

Micah 6:1b commands a single individual to stand up and present the case of law that the mountains (and hills) and foundations of the earth are to decide. Judging from 6:1a, the one issuing the command is the Lord. Who is to "rise and plead?" This could be God's instruction to the prophet to get up and prosecute the case. It seems more likely, however, that this is God's challenge to Israel. The covenant between God and Israel was at the breaking point. The leaders of the nation were guilty of coveting (2:2); worshiping other gods (1:7; 6:16); stealing (2:2; 6:11); and even committing murder (3:10); all the while displaying an inappropriate use of the Lord's name (3:11b). The situation can be compared to one nation breaking a treaty with another, stronger nation or to marriage partners breaking a marriage covenant.

Israel was not unaware of the consequences of a broken covenant (see Deuteronomy 28:15–68). God challenged Israel to make a formal accusation showing how God had failed to keep the covenant. God even convened the court so Israel could have its day in court. The people of God refused to speak, however. They remained silent in spite of the command to present their grievances.

> Out of the despair of being unable to do anything great, we often fail to do anything at all.

God would not let the case drop. God had no intention of settling this out of court. If the people would not argue their case (6:1), then God would carry the litigation forward (6:2). The word translated "controversy" is a technical, legal term. It goes beyond a simple indictment to include the whole legal process of resolving the dispute between two parties. God began the trial by taking the seat of the defendant rather than the place of prosecutor. God spoke as one wrongfully accused, not as an accuser. God in effect asked (6:3), *What have I done wrong? Have I asked too much of you?* God's self-defense showed that far from oppressing the people, he had delivered them from oppression. Rather than burdening them, God had freed them from the burden of their slavery (6:4). Moses, Aaron, and Miriam were God's gifts to the people. Through Moses, God revealed clearly the guidelines for living within God's will. Through Aaron, God provided a line of priests to help Israel deal with its sin. Through Miriam, God demonstrated that women have an equal place within the kingdom.

God's blessing of Israel extended beyond the Exodus from Egypt. It included the entrance into the Promised Land (6:5; see Numbers 22—24). On the journey to the Promised Land, forces outside of Israel sought to harm the people. God reminded the court of Balak, the king of Moab, who tried to hire the prophet Balaam to bring down curses on Israel. The prophet understood that the Lord was with Israel. Thus Balaam at first refused to have anything to do with the plot. Under further pressure from King Balak, Balaam decided to give it a try. Balaam may have been blinded by the salary the king offered, but his donkey was not blind to the Lord's presence. In the end, at the Lord's prompting, Balaam could not curse Israel but rather blessed the people four times (Num. 24:10–15). Indeed, in spite of Israel's own sin, God led the people from Shittim (the last camp on the eastern side of the Jordan River) to Gilgal (the first camp on its western bank inside the Promised Land), by way of dry ground (Joshua 3—4).

God recited this history in order that Israel "may know the saving acts of the Lord" (Micah 6:5). God was doing more than teaching a history lesson or reminding the people of what they already knew in their heads. The Hebrew verb translated "know" has the significance of *to experience, to know deeply and intimately.* The purpose of God's speech was to share with Israel his saving love that had been evident from the beginning of the nation's life. These events in the salvation history of God's people were just some of God's acts of grace that we as Christians believe reached their climax in the cross of Jesus Christ.

> The covenant . . . was a relationship with God and the community of faith made possible first of all by God's grace at work in the events of history.

The covenant was more than a list of rules for Israel to follow. It was a relationship with God and the community of faith made possible first of all by God's grace at work in the events of history. The point of the lawsuit was to warn Israel that the people's actions were putting this life-giving relationship with God in danger. *To know you deeply and intimately — in a real true love relationship*

## The Question (6:6–7)

A single voice speaks in verse 6. Was this an individual sincerely raising the question of how to restore this saving relationship with God? Or, could this be the prophet Micah putting words filled with satire into the mouths of a silent audience in order to set up the powerful declaration of Micah 6:8? It could be Micah's way of condemning the whole religious system of ritual and ceremony, which missed the practical, living, relational aspects of life in the covenant community. Nevertheless, let's give the voice the benefit of the doubt. Let's hear this as one person's hesitant but searching question, an authentic, honest response to the prophet's preaching (6:6): "With what shall I come before the Lord?"

The individual offered suggestions that demonstrate an amazing sense of selflessness. The first suggestion is a burnt offering, a type of sacrifice in which the whole animal is burned on the altar before the Lord. Other methods of sacrifice allowed the worshiper to share in a meal as part of the service, but this method offered nothing to the individual. That the sacrificial animal would be a year-old calf made it an even more costly sacrifice,

# Covenant Lawsuit

Many texts in the prophetic writings in addition to Micah 6:1–8 imitate court-room speech (see Isaiah 1:2–3; Hosea 4:1–6; 12:2–14; Jeremiah 2:4–13). Some scholars have called these texts covenant lawsuits because the issue at stake is the covenant relation between Israel and the Lord. The Hebrew word *rib* (pronounced *reev)* means *controversy, complaint, lawsuit,* or *litigation.* In its verbal form the word means "to argue a case."

While there is a great variety in these examples of lawsuits, they do demonstrate a dramatic quality because of the personal involvement of the Lord in the courtroom scene, and because of the comprehensive scope of the trial. The trial and its outcome affect the whole people of God.

but one still within the realm of possibility for many worshipers. The suggestions quickly escalate, however, to gifts that would be possible only for kings: "Will the Lord be pleased with thousands of rams, with ten thousands of rivers of oil?" (6:7a; see David, 1 Chronicles 29:21; and Solomon, 1 Kings 3:4). Was a pleasing relationship with God available only to the rich and royal? Or did it require a willingness to go beyond what anyone's money can buy and come only at the cost of child sacrifice (6:7b)?

These possibilities are raised, evidently, with the full willingness to carry them out if necessary. The response to the prophet's message was: *What is it going to take? How much is it going to cost me?* That question, however, is the wrong question. It is not "With *what* shall I come . . ." as much as the question is: "O Lord, *who* may abide in your tent? *Who* may dwell on your holy hill?" (Psalm 15:1, italics for emphasis; see also Psalm 24:3).

God's interest is not in things, but in people. The power of worship does not lie in the extravagance of either the offering we give or the ritual we perform. Micah insisted that worship is powerless and meaningless if it has as its basis a human effort to appease, impress, or bribe God. Worship is one aspect of a personal response to God's prior loving, saving activity, and cannot be divorced from other aspects such as personal commitment to justice, integrity, and honesty.

## The Answer (6:8)

Does Micah 6:8 answer the question of Micah 6:6–7? The question asked was how to approach God. The answer is about "what is good." "What is good" is a saving relationship with God, and that is also the intent of the question, *With what may I approach God?* The individual wants to know whether this relationship could be established by means of extravagant gifts beyond the means of but a few or even beyond the bounds of our imagination. The answer given in verse 8 directs the individual to refocus the question as a giving of self rather than a giving of things. *as a living sacrifice*

> *Micah insisted that worship is powerless and meaningless if it has as its basis a human effort to appease, impress, or bribe God.*

The answer was not directed only to the individual who spoke Micah 6:6–7, but it was addressed to each person who was willing to stand responsibly before God: "O Mortal" (6:8). The beginning of verse 8 can be translated as either "He has told you," or *It has been shown to you.* The verbal form means literally: *It has been made conspicuous.* Something can be made conspicuous by telling or by demonstration.

The main point is that we human beings are not left to wonder or work out an answer for ourselves; God has revealed the answer to us. When Micah declares that what is good has been revealed to us, he does not have in mind a particular verse or selection of laws in the Bible. He is saying that God has communicated the possibility of a personal relationship with himself by means of the whole saving activity of God.

This is good news. We do not have to speculate on "what is good" (6:8). God has clearly shown us the answer.

"What is good" is also *what the Lord requires of us* (6:8b). The basic meaning of the verb translated "require" (6:8) is *to seek.* What follows is the statement of an expectation. This is what the Lord is looking for from us. This is what can be expected of one who lives in right relationship with God.

The prophet then described in three phrases what the Lord was looking for in the lives of his people. The first phrase is: "to do justice." In Micah 3:1 the prophet had complained that Judah's rulers did not "know" justice. That is, they did not demonstrate a deep, personal commitment to the right. The demand is that commitment to justice be shown through the practice of seeking to relieve the troubles of those who are oppressed and to

> *As individual believers, we are to demonstrate a teachable spirit in our daily walk with God.*

bring healing to broken relationships. "To do justice" is not merely to obey the letter of the law but to effect the practices of a fair social order.

"To do justice" is to make God's will actual and real in the setting in which one lives.

The second phrase is "to love kindness." The Hebrew word *chesed* is difficult to translate into English with just one or two words. Modern attempts include kindness, mercy, steadfast love, and loyalty. The words "justice" (*mishpat*) and "kindness" form a common word pair in the Old Testament (see Hosea 12:6; Zechariah 7:9). So it should not surprise us that the two phrases "to do justice" and "to love kindness" are two ways of expressing the same thing, but the second phrase deepens the meaning of the first. The extra depth of meaning is conveyed on the one hand by the use of the verb "to love" as the parallel expression for "to do." The mere practice of justice is not enough, but there must be a heartfelt affection for such a practice. Furthermore, "to love kindness" (*chesed)* is an expression of loyalty to a covenant, a sense of being part of a community, and therefore a sense of solidarity that willingly makes common cause with others for the good of all. Thus the community is bound together in goodwill as well as right acts.

> *If we are attentive and receptive to God's guidance in our daily commitment to him, we will be empowered to lovingly practice justice and mercy.*

The third phrase, "to walk humbly with your God," also expresses "what is good" from a different perspective rather than simply being the third item on a list of distinct requirements. "To walk," of course, is a figurative expression for *to have as a way of life.* Life is pictured as a journey, and what is good in life is to share that journey with God. Notice the personal element involved in that journey. The journey is "with *your* God" (italics for emphasis). This shared, personal journey, however, is to be marked by a specific attitude. One is to walk "humbly." The idea seems to be *to walk attentively, alertly with God.* The arrogant are unteachable. A right relationship with God that results in the practice of justice motivated by a heartfelt love of community is possible only when we demonstrate a teachable spirit.

The answer to the question of what it takes to have a personal, saving relationship with the Lord found in Micah 6:8 can be paraphrased as follows: *It has been revealed to you, O human being, what is good. What does the Lord look for in you but to practice just living, to do so out of a loving commitment to the whole community of God, and to accomplish this by walking attentively with your God?*

166

## Relevance for Today

As individual believers, we are to demonstrate a teachable spirit in our daily walk with God. We need to be alert to God's guidance to make a difference for good as citizens in this land. Nevertheless, the place where we can be a real witness of God's way of life is through the building of that unique community called the church.

As a congregation, we can decide together to make the church a laboratory where our treatment of one another is justice in action, whether we are male or female, affluent or impoverished, white or black or Hispanic or any other race. This true community of justice cannot be one of outward behavior only, but our actions must be an expression of a shared inner affection for the community as a whole. The only possible source for this combination of emotion and act is God. If we are attentive and receptive to God's guidance in our daily commitment to him, we will be empowered to lovingly practice justice and mercy.

*We do not have to speculate on "what is good" (6:8).*

## QUESTIONS

1. Are there any indications in the life of the church today that there is a rupture in our relationship with God? What are they?

2. What are some of the ways people try to establish a relationship to God through their own efforts? Are these efforts any more effective than those mentioned in Micah 6:6–7?

3. What responses do you think the general population would make if we asked this question: "What is good for a human being?" How are these responses helpful? How do they fall short of God's response?

4. What are some specific ways to practice justice?

5. How can one express a commitment to kindness?

6. What are some characteristics of an attentive walk with the Lord?

# Our Next New Study
### (Available for use beginning September 2003)

## *Letters to the PHILIPPIANS, COLOSSIANS, and THESSALONIANS*

### PHILIPPIANS: REJOICING IN CHRIST

| | | |
|---|---|---|
| Lesson 1 | Look at Life Positively | Philippians 1:1–26 |
| Lesson 2 | Live a Life Worthy of the Gospel | Philippians 1:27—2:15 |
| Lesson 3 | Make a Difference with Your Life | Philippians 2:19–30 |
| Lesson 4 | Keep Focused on Knowing Christ | Philippians 3:2–14 |
| Lesson 5 | Live with Genuine Joy | Philippians 4:2–19 |

### COLOSSIANS: CHRIST OVER ALL

| | | |
|---|---|---|
| Lesson 6 | Who's Number One? | Colossians 1:1–23 |
| Lesson 7 | Lose the Rules | Colossians 2:6–23 |
| Lesson 8 | Live It Up! | Colossians 3:1—4:1 |

### THE THESSALONIAN LETTERS: FAITH, LOVE, AND HOPE

| | | |
|---|---|---|
| Lesson 9 | A Church for Which to Be Grateful | 1 Thessalonians 1:1–10; 2:13–14 |
| Lesson 10 | Leadership That Inspires Followers | 1 Thessalonians 2:1–12; 5:12–13 |
| Lesson 11 | Instructions for Lives That Please God | 1 Thessalonians 4:1–12; 5:14–21 |
| Lesson 12 | Hope for Loved Ones and Ourselves | 1 Thessalonians 4:13—5:11 |
| Lesson 13 | Faith That Works in the Workplace | 2 Thessalonians 3:6–13 |

Additional Resources for Studying Philippians[1]
Fred B. Craddock. *Philippians.* Interpretation: A Bible Commentary for Teaching and Preaching. Atlanta: John Knox Press, 1985.

Morna D. Hooker. "Philippians." *The New Interpreter's Bible.* Volume XI. Nashville: Abingdon Press, 2000.

Ralph P. Martin. *Philippians.* Revised edition. The Tyndale New Testament Commentaries. Grand Rapids, Michigan: William B. Eerdmans Publishing Company, 1987.

Frank Stagg. "Philippians." *The Broadman Bible Commentary.* Volume 11. Nashville, Tennessee: Broadman Press, 1971.

Additional Resources for Studying Colossians
Andrew T. Lincoln. "Colossians." *The New Interpreter's Bible.* Volume XI. Nashville: Abingdon Press, 2000.

R.E.O. White. "Colossians." *The Broadman Bible Commentary.* Volume 11. Nashville, Tennessee: Broadman Press, 1971.

Additional Resources for Studying 1 and 2 Thessalonians
F.F. Bruce. *1 & 2 Thessalonians.* Word Biblical Commentary. Volume 45. Waco, Texas: Word Books, Inc., 1982.

Beverly Roberts Gaventa. *First and Second Thessalonians.* Interpretation: A Bible Commentary for Teaching and Preaching. Louisville: John Knox Press, 1998.

Herschel H. Hobbs. "1—2 Thessalonians." *The Broadman Bible Commentary.* Volume 11. Nashville, Tennessee: Broadman Press, 1971.

Abraham Smith. "The First Letter to the Thessalonians" and "The Second Letter to the Thessalonians." *The New Interpreter's Bible.* Volume XI. Nashville: Abingdon Press, 2000.

# NOTES

1. Listing a book does not imply full agreement by the writers or BAPTISTWAY PRESS® with all of its comments.

# How to Order More Bible Study Materials

It's easy! Just fill in the following information. (Note: when the *Teaching Guide* is priced at $2.45, the *Teaching Guide* includes Bible comments for teachers.)
🌵 = Texas specific

| Title of item | Price | Quantity | Cost |
|---|---|---|---|
| **This Issue:** | | | |
| Amos, Hosea, Micah—*Study Guide* | $1.95 | | |
| Amos, Hosea, Micah—*Large Print Study Guide* | $1.95 | | |
| Amos, Hosea, Micah—*Teaching Guide* | $2.45 | | |
| **Previous Issues Available:** | | | |
| God's Message in the Old Testament—*Study Guide* 🌵 | $1.95 | | |
| God's Message in the Old Testament—*Teaching Guide* 🌵 | $1.95 | | |
| Genesis 12—50: Family Matters—*Study Guide* | $1.95 | | |
| Genesis 12—50: Family Matters—*Large Print Study Guide* | $1.95 | | |
| Genesis 12—50: Family Matters—*Teaching Guide* | $2.45 | | |
| Good News in the New Testament—*Study Guide* 🌵 | $1.95 | | |
| Good News in the New Testament—*Large Print Study Guide* 🌵 | $1.95 | | |
| Good News in the New Testament—*Teaching Guide* 🌵 | $2.45 | | |
| Isaiah and Jeremiah—*Study Guide* | $1.95 | | |
| Isaiah and Jeremiah—*Large Print Study Guide* | $1.95 | | |
| Isaiah and Jeremiah—*Teaching Guide* | $2.45 | | |
| Matthew: Jesus As the Fulfillment of God's Promises—*Study Guide* 🌵 | $1.95 | | |
| Matthew: Jesus As the Fulfillment of God's Promises—*Large Print Study Guide* 🌵 | $1.95 | | |
| Matthew: Jesus As the Fulfillment of God's Promises—*Teaching Guide* 🌵 | $2.45 | | |
| Jesus in the Gospel of Mark—*Study Guide* | $1.95 | | |
| Jesus in the Gospel of Mark—*Large Print Study Guide* | $1.95 | | |
| Jesus in the Gospel of Mark—*Teaching Guide* | $2.45 | | |
| Gospel of John—*Study Guide* | $1.95 | | |
| Gospel of John—*Large Print Study Guide* | $1.95 | | |
| Gospel of John—*Teaching Guide* | $2.45 | | |
| Acts: Sharing God's Good News with Everyone—*Study Guide* 🌵 | $1.95 | | |
| Acts: Sharing God's Good News with Everyone —*Teaching Guide* 🌵 | $1.95 | | |
| Romans: Good News for a Troubled World—*Study Guide* 🌵 | $1.95 | | |
| Romans: Good News for a Troubled World—*Teaching Guide* 🌵 | $1.95 | | |
| 1 Corinthians—*Study Guide* | $1.95 | | |
| 1 Corinthians—*Large Print Study Guide* | $1.95 | | |
| 1 Corinthians—*Teaching Guide* | $2.45 | | |
| Galatians: By Grace Through Faith, and Ephesians: God's Plan and Our Response—*Study Guide* 🌵 | $1.95 | | |
| Galatians: By Grace Through Faith, and Ephesians: God's Plan and Our Response—*Large Print Study Guide* 🌵 | $1.95 | | |
| Galatians: By Grace Through Faith, and Ephesians: God's Plan and Our Response—*Teaching Guide* 🌵 | $2.45 | | |
| Hebrews and James—*Study Guide* | $1.95 | | |
| Hebrews and James—*Large Print Study Guide* | $1.95 | | |
| Hebrews and James—*Teaching Guide* | $2.45 | | |
| **Coming for use beginning September 2003** | | | |
| Philippians, Colossians, Thessalonians—*Study Guide* | $1.95 | | |
| Philippians, Colossians, Thessalonians—*Large Print Study Guide* | $1.95 | | |
| Philippians, Colossians, Thessalonians—*Teaching Guide* | $2.45 | | |

## Beliefs Important to Baptists

| | | | |
|---|---|---|---|
| Who in the World Are Baptists, Anyway? (one lesson) | $ .45 | _____ | _____ |
| Who in the World Are Baptists, Anyway?—Teacher's Edition | $ .55 | _____ | _____ |
| Beliefs Important to Baptists: I (four lessons) | $1.35 | _____ | _____ |
| Beliefs Important to Baptists: I—Teacher's Edition | $1.75 | _____ | _____ |
| Beliefs Important to Baptists: II (four lessons) | $1.35 | _____ | _____ |
| Beliefs Important to Baptists: II—Teacher's Edition | $1.75 | _____ | _____ |
| Beliefs Important to Baptists: III (four lessons) | $1.35 | _____ | _____ |
| Beliefs Important to Baptists: III—Teacher's Edition | $1.75 | _____ | _____ |
| Beliefs Important to Baptists—Study Guide (one-volume edition; includes all lessons) | $2.35 | _____ | _____ |
| Beliefs Important to Baptists—Teaching Guide (one-volume edition; includes all lessons) | $1.95 | _____ | _____ |

*Charges for standard shipping service:

| | |
|---|---|
| Subtotal up to $20.00 | $3.95 |
| Subtotal $20.01—$50.00 | $4.95 |
| Subtotal $50.01—$100.00 | 10% of subtotal |
| Subtotal $100.01 and up | 8% of subtotal |

Please allow three weeks for standard delivery. For express shipping service: Call 1-866-249-1799 for information on additional charges.

Subtotal _____

Shipping* _____

TOTAL _____

Number of FREE copies of *Brief Basics for Texas Baptists* needed for leading adult Sunday School department periods _____

Your name

Phone

Your church

Date Ordered

Mailing address

City

State     Zip code

**MAIL** this form with your check for the total amount to
BAPTISTWAY PRESS
Baptist General Convention of Texas
333 North Washington
Dallas, TX 75246-1798
(Make checks to "Baptist Executive Board.")

OR, **FAX** your order anytime to: 214-828-5187, and we will bill you.

OR, **CALL** your order toll-free: 1-866-249-1799 (8:30 a.m.–5:00 p.m., M-F), and we will bill you.

OR, **E-MAIL** your order to our internet e-mail address: baptistway@bgct.org, and we will bill you.

We look forward to receiving your order! Thank you!